REFLECTIONS OF A SEASONED SOUL

True stories of transformation experienced by an inspired hospice nurse and impassioned spiritual traveler.

Jean Keegan Daly

BALBOA.
PRESS
A DIVISION OF HAY HOUSE

Ms. Dorothy Meyers

Dear Dorothy,
My long time friend I
hand many happy memories and
funny ones too, with you! My
wishes for you from my heart
are that you continue to
shine your beautiful soul
light as it guides you on your
path with comfort, peace, love and
beauty.
With loving blessings
to you always,
Jean

Copyright © 2017 Jean Keegan Daly.

All rights reserved. No part of this book may be used or reproduced by any means, graphic, electronic, or mechanical, including photocopying, recording, taping or by any information storage retrieval system without the written permission of the author except in the case of brief quotations embodied in critical articles and reviews.

Balboa Press books may be ordered through booksellers or by contacting:

Balboa Press
A Division of Hay House
1663 Liberty Drive
Bloomington, IN 47403
www.balboapress.com
1 (877) 407-4847

Because of the dynamic nature of the Internet, any web addresses or links contained in this book may have changed since publication and may no longer be valid. The views expressed in this work are solely those of the author and do not necessarily reflect the views of the publisher, and the publisher hereby disclaims any responsibility for them.

The author of this book does not dispense medical advice or prescribe the use of any technique as a form of treatment for physical, emotional, or medical problems without the advice of a physician, either directly or indirectly. The intent of the author is only to offer information of a general nature to help you in your quest for emotional and spiritual well-being. In the event you use any of the information in this book for yourself, which is your constitutional right, the author and the publisher assume no responsibility for your actions.

Any people depicted in stock imagery provided by Thinkstock are models, and such images are being used for illustrative purposes only.
Certain stock imagery © Thinkstock.

Print information available on the last page.

ISBN: 978-1-5043-7569-6 (sc)
ISBN: 978-1-5043-7571-9 (hc)
ISBN: 978-1-5043-7570-2 (e)

Library of Congress Control Number: 2017902808

Balboa Press rev. date: 03/31/2017

Praise for Reflections of a Seasoned Soul

Reflections of a Seasoned Soul by Jean Daly is one of those rare books that every reader will immediately recognize as a direct gift from the Divine. Jean has generously shared both the successes and the many trials and hardships of her impassioned life quest to understand and incorporate her spiritual self into everyday living... so that all of us may have an easier time understanding and succeeding in our own journeys. This book should be required reading for anyone hoping to live a life of value. As a journalist my own quest has been to discover truly inspired people and their messages that resonate broadly for the rest of us. Jean Daly is at the top of my list. Her life work as a registered nurse and her experiences with dying patients in Hospice gives her unique insights into what we all are doing on this earth. Moreover, Jean's experiences with Angelic beings gives us all an understanding and appreciation of God's unimaginable love for us, and what is possible when we strive to really understand our place in His wonderful gift that we call life. If you read one book this year, make it Reflections of a Seasoned Soul.

—Ted Yacucci,
Professor of Mass Communications and Journalism,
Delaware State University

CONTENTS

CONTENTS

DEDICATION

With my love and heartfelt appreciation I dedicate this book to my beloved parents, Jim and Betty Keegan, who are now with us in spirit, and to my loving family, most especially to my cherished sons, Dennis and Shaun Daly, who saw me through the challenging journey of my soul. In reading these true stories may you all have a deeper understanding of my heart and my soul and may this deepen and expand our love, our commitment, and our unity with each other and with the Spirit of God.

MY GRATITUDE

I most sincerely and warmly thank everyone who so graciously gave of their time, their energy, their insights, their suggestions, their technical skills, their encouragement, their love and support to me during the writing of this book.

These include all my family, friends and colleagues.

To those who so willingly gave me their reviewing and editing assistance I particularly thank long time special friends; Mary Ann Jenkins, Nancy Burgas, Shirley Roberts, and Pam Jones.

For their hands-on technical assistance, I particularly thank special family members; my sister and brother-in-law, Lori and Bruce Beyerle, my brothers, Tom Keegan and Buddy Keegan, and my nephew, Craig Beyerle. You have each lovingly contributed to the development of my book in several unique ways.

MaryAnn was a student in my earliest meditation classes and became a kindred soul traveler who was with me during my amazing Monroe Institute experiences. Throughout the years MaryAnn has listened with loving attention to many of my stories and gave me the push I needed to finally write my book. She offered her helpful idea of writing my chapters in a sectional story format and gave me good constructive ideas that contributed to the book's flow.

Nancy graciously reviewed one of my lengthy chapters and gave me her helpful constructive ideas that expanded understanding of certain story details. Nancy also generously offered me a beautiful private space in her home in New Mexico if I ever needed to write in solitude.

Pam and Shirley so kindly read my first story at different times during its completion process. Shirley also read other story parts that I felt needed review. These two friends each offered me their keen insights, beneficial comments and positive personal responses.

Buddy called me every single week to offer his support, encouragement, love and belief in me. He offered very helpful feedback with reorganizing one of my chapters and focused me when I became distracted by the weight of it all.

Tom, Lori, Bruce, and Craig were so helpful to me in their adept applications of technical support with my computer and with editing and filing issues. Tom also came several times to my home and spent hours repairing issues with my computer and printing systems. Lori encouraged and supported me many times.

My gratitude also goes out to Ted Yacucci whom I met at a meeting during the same time as the inception of my manuscript. He enthusiastically encouraged me to write and offered his help with some of my technical research.

To each of you I am deeply grateful for generously assisting me with your time and energy, your skill, your caring, your love, your support and your belief in me.

I am also very thankful to every single one of my dearest family and close friends who often inquired about my progress, reassured me, offered comfort when I felt overwhelmed, and told me of their genuine excitement to read my book. You all gave me encouragement to believe that this often arduous undertaking would be valuable to the world. I lovingly thank you very much.

PREFACE

Dear Readers,

Thank you for choosing to explore the personal experiences that I share with you in this, my first book. These stories and insights reflect my soulful quest for the fullest truth of my purpose here in this life. At its beginning I could not have imagined how my journey would unfold in the surprising and unusual ways it did. During times of my most difficult challenges and strongest emotions, I felt literally lifted up and steered toward decisions that, even through my doubt and fear, I knew were right. First though, I had to learn how to deal with and how to quiet my ego-self in order to determine that the guidance I received was clearly God-sent. Throughout the many years of my journey I relied on prayer, hope, faith, strength, trust, love and positive attitude to get me through. I promise you with my deepest honesty and integrity that every story, every word in this book is my truth. It has taken me a long time to finish it as I have struggled with much hesitancy and anxiety in risking judgment, criticism, and invalidation from others. Yet, for many years I have been repeatedly inspired and safely guided in so many ways to acknowledge and share my experiences. My fervent hope is that they will inspire and assist those who realize that they too are on a personal journey of the soul, a journey which expands human consciousness. This expansion allows us to wake up from the illusions of ego and separation, to see ourselves united within the Whole and actively remember and live from our true inherent Divine Nature. I believe this awareness motivates us to live life authentically within the incredible power of Divine Love. Every day is an opportunity to nurture and reinforce this knowing. The experience is powerful and enriching. I wish it for you in your own way and time. It is also my hope to inspire those of you with similar stories to find the courage within yourselves to share them. The world is in great need of the healing power and the truth of Love. May you always know and feel the presence of the Divine and be showered and guided by Its loving grace.

God bless each of you.

With love and gratitude,
Jean Keegan Daly

Opening Words to Theme from the Movie "Mahogany"
Sung by Diana Ross

"DO YOU KNOW WHERE YOU'RE GOING TO?

**DO YOU LIKE THE THINGS THAT
LIFE IS SHOWING YOU?**

WHERE ARE YOU GOING TO?

DO YOU KNOW?"

The words of this song resonated with me as soon as I heard them.
The following pages of my personal story tell why...

Stepping into the Journey

Sometime long ago I learned that personal fear and anxiety come from not living up to your own potential. I think fear also slithers around inside those who do not know their life purpose, or may wonder about it but do not know how to discover it. Some are disconnected from their core essence, the Spiritual Source that provides everything needed to discover and fulfill the purpose for which we each came into this world. Some choose to NOT discover their purpose for many reasons. Others think their purpose is supposed to be of a singular dimension, yet they suspect and fear that it is so much more. This last meaning applied to me.

My first story sets the stage for the many experiences through which I traveled on my journey to discover more about God, life's conditions and meanings, and to understand myself with the truth of my own spiritual nature and its full purpose in my life. I could not have imagined just how complex, multidimensional, and multifaceted that evolutionary process would be. Since the age of five years I knew that I wanted to be a nurse, a wife and a mother, in that order. My life plan was supposed to unfold smoothly and easily according to the design that only an innocent, immature child's mind can devise. I was not prepared for all the complicated developments and detours to come.

I'll start at the very beginning. It was early January, 1946.

Being the first born of six children, I arrived as a "feet first" breech birth baby. Obviously, I was ready to get going in the world! In the patriarchal society of the 1940's, boys were supposed to be the ones in charge so it was preferred that a boy be a family's first born. In adopting this generational attitude my young parents, ages 20 and 21, fresh from the Navy where they had met and married, desired and expected their first child, born a year later, to be a boy. Mom told me that they hadn't even chosen a name for a girl. But there I was, a first born, feet first girl, ready to go! Right from the start I acquired my parents' expectation of being the leader and to always set good examples to everyone, especially to my future younger siblings.

By the age of 4 years I had two baby brothers, whom I eagerly and daily helped Mom care for. It felt natural for me to want to be Mom's little helper and to soothe and calm the babies. I was proud to contribute and learn from my mom to be responsible. All of this felt fun and comfortable then. I also began school at age 4 years even though my 5th birthday was 3 months past the cut-off date for school entrance. I vividly remember playing school teacher at home while pretending that my baby brothers, along with my doll and teddy bear, were my students. I felt quite grown up, indeed.

During my time in kindergarten our wonderful family dog became very ill and was suddenly taken away by the dog catcher, a title well known at that time. I clearly remember that event. My mom was sobbing as the man removed Teddy from our small veteran's home. We both stood at the door saying goodbye to our beloved family pet. I had no idea that he would not return. Of course Mom knew that he would die because he had the disease of distemper. My mom tried to explain this to me through her tears. It was my first experience with the meanings of death, loss and grief.

My fun role as helper to Mom shifted in that moment as I witnessed her grieving and mourning. She was always so busy taking care of us and our home and now she had to deal with this. Looking up at her that day I reached out to comfort my mother, hug her and somehow help her feel better. I had never before seen my mother cry or be so sad. Even at my young age I somehow knew that Teddy's loss was also representative of other unexpressed losses and suppressed pain that my mother suffered. All I wanted to do was be there for my mom and make her feel better. That day, at the tender age of 5, I instinctively knew that helping and soothing others would be my lifelong work. My Christmas wish from Santa that year was for a nurse's kit. He left it under the tree and I was thrilled.

As time passed two more brothers and a baby sister

joined the family and I became even more responsible as the serious-minded older sister of five younger siblings. Starting at age 11, which was an eventful year for me, I was left in charge to babysit whenever needed. My sister had not yet been born and my four brothers were then ages 1 to 10 years. My role as babysitter did not sit well with my "age closest" brothers who thought I was bossy. In retrospect I'm sure that it is how I really appeared to them, yet the truth was that as much as I demonstrated feeling capable of being in charge, I was always scared. I wanted to do a good job, do it "right," especially to please my parents, and feel important and needed in this large family. I tried to figure out how to balance such responsibility with what I thought it meant to be grown up, poised and composed. It took some years of maturing for me to realize how my brothers must have felt at that time with a girl being in charge of them and telling them, with a dose of superior attitude, what to do and how to behave.

Making my duties even more serious were the facts that I was the daughter of a well known police officer and we lived five houses away from the Catholic Church and school which we all attended. That made the nuns and priests particularly alert to any infractions of the many rules that I, as the eldest child, was especially required to strictly follow. Corporal punishment, in both family and school environments, was regularly meted out especially for disobedience and disrespect. This was considered normal and necessary by the social patriarchy of that era.

Phrases like "stop that crying or I'll give you something to cry about" and "children are to be seen and not heard" and "because I said so" were frequent commands. It was acceptable for neighbors and other known adults to become strict disciplinarians if they witnessed infractions of the rules. There was no getting away with anything!

When I was 11 years old we moved into our new home, built singlehandedly by my father to accommodate our growing family. He often had to supplement our finances with two extra jobs in addition to working rotating shifts at the police department. It was difficult on all of us and especially so on our mom, particularly because all of her family lived quite far away. Although Dad worked very hard, he had a sense of humor and would tell silly jokes. He taught himself to play guitar to relax. I loved when he played and invited me to sing along with him. I particularly enjoyed times when he played at family gatherings and he and I sang together.

My mother was very skilled in cooking, cleaning, sewing, mending and running a clean, well organized and functional household. Mom taught me to do all those things for which I am very grateful. We all had daily chores and time was not to be wasted in doing them. My mother had a wonderful talent for artistic design. This was evident all through the house, in her flower gardens, and in the clothing and Halloween costumes she made for us. Mom was always in motion. I don't ever remember her really relaxing. She didn't believe in it because she said there was too much to get done. As she worked every day in our home, Mom often sang along to the radio and I enjoyed listening to her. My parents had many friends with whom they would attend police department related social events. They were excellent dancers which I thought was wonderful and wanted to emulate. So Dad taught me to dance when I was age 11. Of course because of such busyness in our family there very few times my Dad and I could do this. However, my love of music, dancing and singing became my passions and continue to be so today. To me these all represent fun, freedom, creative expression and joy; feelings I longed to express more often in my youth.

Although I remember the music, the overall dynamic of our home was mostly serious with much structure. I knew my parents loved me and were committed to doing what they believed was right in raising me with strict rules. Still, I was a very sensitive and sentimental girl who very deeply felt emotions regardless of whether they were my own or another's, always feeling sorry for anyone who was sad or in pain or getting into trouble. I wanted everyone to be relaxed and happy. I took everything to heart, often being tearful at things others would not be, and feeling confused and misunderstood. I frequently felt stressed and hyper-vigilant, yet in that era children were not supposed to feel that way because they were considered care-free children. I had a visionary mind with different ideas about some of the rigid beliefs I was taught at home, in school, in church, and in society. I knew I was to follow the rules yet there were times as a teenager I tried to challenge some of those beliefs by asking pointed questions and trying to give my viewpoint with its rationale. I wanted to be listened to with my opinion being at least considered somewhat valuable. However, my comments were most often viewed as "talking back." Of course I did not think so, yet that trait got me into trouble and I was repeatedly chastised for it.

In John Bradshaw's book "The Family," the eldest child is considered the Hero Child, the one responsible for bringing honor and pride to the family. Of course I didn't read that book until adulthood, yet in my youth I automatically knew that was my top job. However, I wanted to expand that concept through new ideas that I thought would bring even more honor to our family.

One idea I had began with the fact that I loved and valued conversations. So I suggested that we have regular family meetings with us children being free to say (respectfully, of course) what we thought and felt about certain rules and punishments and be allowed to offer reasonable alternatives. Also, that we have calm, relaxed dinner times where we could be allowed to talk and focus only on each one's successes and good qualities. In presenting those ideas to my parents I was frustrated that my efforts to change things (in my mind, to improve things) were not welcomed. It was late 1950's and early 1960's. I was still the child, the rules were the rules, and I was expected to accept and follow them without question and without any expression of anger. This applied to school, church, and social situations as well. My failed attempt to step outside the box and become an open-minded progressive leader in the family was disappointing and confusing for me as an adolescent girl. I felt that there was some deeper part of myself that had been restricted and was longing to be known and expressed. It was something I felt was important yet as a teenager, I was unable to really put that into words. So I kept recommitting myself to be the good daughter who did what she was told and be the example setter to my younger siblings that my parents expected me to be.

I eventually realized that the rigid structure my parents held for us children really did serve a good purpose. It created a foundation of safety and capability in the world as well as an environment within which I learned important core values, such as belief in God, respect, honesty, dependability, accountability, and a good work ethic. I will forever be grateful to my parents for instilling those values.

It's not surprising how my adolescent characteristic of talking and explaining in great detail, followed me into adulthood. I think it became an automatic default to do what I was denied in childhood. However, that trait with my accompanying exuberance, was sometimes annoying even to myself as well as to others, especially the "just give me the bottom line" folks who found my details exasperating. On the other hand, my keen sensitivity and caring made me an attentive and empathetic listener. All of this was very helpful throughout my adult career and is still true about me today...the back and forth flow of talking and sharing, being quiet and listening. At times it can be a challenge to know exactly which to do when, depending on the person and circumstance. I don't always figure that out in the moment!

While growing up I always felt, both inside and outside the family, quite protective of my siblings and I very staunchly defended them to anyone who might have dared to be harsh to them or critical of them. My favorite part of being the older sister was when I played the role of nurse. Any bossiness I showed as babysitter-in-charge melted into nurturing comforter as I tried to tend to my siblings when they were sick or injured or needed support and encouragement. I most dearly and deeply loved all my brothers and my only sister who was born, much to my delight, when I was nearly 15 years of age. My love for all my siblings has only deepened over the years.

My desire to help people be comforted and heal continued to grow. I became a hospital volunteer "candy striper" at age 15 and loved it. That rewarding experience propelled me to enter nurses' training at age 17. There was simply no other career consideration for me, although I did at one time entertain the thought of somehow blending this with being a professional teacher or counselor. I didn't know it then, but that career merger was to happen much later in my life. Actually, nursing always involves a manner of teaching and counseling so really, I was doing it all along, being continually interested in the psychology of people as well as the physiology.

Through an accelerated program of 3 years training in 27 grueling months I gained some maturity, did very well in school and became a Registered Nurse. My goal to become a pediatric nurse was fulfilled in the very hospital where I had trained. I was thrilled! My childhood plan was unfolding as I had imagined. At just 20 years of age all was well in the structure of my life. I was a happily in love newlywed, married to a good man whom I had met during my senior year in high school while working at the local luncheonette. I loved nursing, had good friends, close family, my health, devotional belief in God, and a hope to become a mother in the following year. I believed I was all grown up and could handle most anything.

Taking care of children in the hospital setting was rewarding for me. Unlike most of my adult patients, the children possessed a general ability to recover quickly and resume their spunk and cheerfulness. It amazed me that they could be so sick one day and out enjoying the ward's playroom a day or two later. I've always loved the natural upbeat spirit and spontaneity of children and I interacted well with them.

In the mid 1960's a popular TV show, "The Flintstones," provided the backdrop for getting the children to participate in accepting the dreaded "shot." I would tell them that in order to make them well again I needed to give them a shot that would feel like a pinch or a sting. I would make it happen really fast and then it would be over. Of course the kids didn't want this shot so I made a deal with them. We would both shout "yabadabadoo" over and over just like TV's cartoon character Fred Flintstone, and see which one of us could yell the loudest. But there was one rule. They had to stay very still and not move until we were done yelling. It worked every single time. They got the shot and we had some fun shouting. This was always followed by a cheer, a hug, and a little reward which could be a story or extra playtime or an allowable treat. I was happy to be a nurse helping those young patients.

One morning while I was working in the pediatric department something unexpected and dreadful happened. There was no warning. A beautiful 12 year old girl had been admitted to the ward as my patient. She was very sick, frail and weak, with a persistent cough, intermittent shortness of breath, and needed oxygen to help her breathe. She was the adopted daughter and only child of devoted immigrant parents who were increasingly upset that after having three days of testing, their daughter was still without a firm diagnosis. Efforts to treat her symptoms by several doctors were unsuccessful.

I tried my best to comfort all of them and I earnestly prayed for a miracle recovery for her. I was sure I'd soon see her "bounce back" as I had witnessed in many other very sick children. Instead, she became more ill despite all the care given her. On the third day as I cradled her head to adjust her pillow and moisten her dry lips, this beautiful child looked at me with her soulful eyes and smiled. The next minute she became very limp and suddenly died in my arms. It was totally unexpected and extremely shocking to me! She had been a patient only three days and we needed more time to help her. Efforts to revive her by both me and the emergency team failed. I could not believe it! How could this happen? I felt devastated. An autopsy revealed aggressive lung cancer that had been hidden from x-ray view. There were no ultrasound or MRI tests in those days. It didn't make any sense to me that this 12 year old child could have lung cancer. Wasn't that an adult disease?

My grandfather had suffered and died from lung cancer three years earlier. He had been a heavy smoker all his life and was sick for a long time. I had a hard time coping with his death, even though it was expected. But this was a child who had seemed quite healthy until a few weeks before her hospitalization. Her doctor had been treating her for a stubborn cold virus. This child's sudden, unexpected death from the undiagnosed disease of lung cancer put me in a whirlwind of emotional turmoil. I felt inadequate to comfort her shocked and grief stricken family. My own feelings overwhelmed me. In my strong sense of responsibility I felt that I somehow had failed her and began to doubt my ability to be a good nurse. In following hospital procedure I remember having to tie a name tag on her toe and transport her body to the morgue, all the while weeping and apologizing to her.

I took several days off from work to process my grief as well as I could. I spent much time praying to understand and accept this tragedy. There had been no nursing school training in how to deal with one's personal grief over the loss of a patient, especially a child. Also, being newly pregnant I worried about my ability to prevent my own child from becoming so sick.

Soon it was time to return to my job responsibilities on the pediatric unit. Although I needed to be externally composed I had to tuck the painful experience of my patient's death in a private pocket within my heart and move on to work again with the children. To help myself I needed to depend on the religion of my childhood which had long ago provided me with a strong foundation of belief in God and the necessity of having faith and trust in God's Will, even when it confused or scared me. I was determined to strengthen my relationship with God and deepen my faith and trust. With that I felt I could give the best and most compassionate care possible to my patients, my family, and anyone else in need for whatever time we were to have together. I began fortifying myself with the realization that each life has its own purposeful order and that I personally have no control over anyone's life or death timeline, including those of my own family. I had to trust in the Divine Order of things. This became my mental mantra. Even so, I had doubts and yearned for a way to make sense of it all. My heart asked questions that my mind could not answer.

As months and years passed I was involved in being a loving, dedicated wife and mother and felt happy and proud to have the privilege of staying home to raise our two sons who were close in age. When our younger son was 3 1/2 years old there was a need for me to return to nursing in part time positions. These helped with family finances, kept me current with healthcare changes, and expanded my nursing role into new areas. I worked with families of children, older teens and adults in various situations and places, including their own homes. Those experiences really opened my awareness to peoples' desperate home life situations that often left them poor, abused, sick, lonely, afraid and sometimes suicidal.

Being in people's homes was especially revealing about their dire situations and personal private hell. My mind swirled with thoughts and questions in trying to understand. As much as I loved being a nurse I was becoming increasingly confused and upset by the presence of people's continual pain, unrelenting distress, and heart-wrenching suffering all around me. What was the purpose of that? Whenever someone's agony could not be relieved, my heart's questions became louder and sharper. What could be the purpose of people, even little children, suffering from poverty, neglect, abuse, violence, pain, debilitating illness, and untimely death? What was the purpose of having that kind of life? Why would some people who were good, kind, hardworking people seem to be singled out to live such a life of struggle, and sometimes have that struggle continue into next generations? It bothered me when some people, whose lives flowed easily with health and wealth, pronounced themselves as being more blessed by God than others. Even though I realized it sounded judgmental of me, I thought they were arrogant to believe they were the "chosen ones." Why would a loving God, the Creator of all, choose to bless only certain people with an easy life?

More questions arose in my mind. Why were people

given only one life? Couldn't they have another chance to live a happy, healthy life? It all seemed so unfair. Where was God in all this? How could this really be God's plan? Even though I was very grateful I often felt guilty for enjoying all that I had in my own life while others were so deprived. Was some sort of chaos really in control of the universe? What could I really trust to remain steady?

My faith and trust in the Divine Order of things was challenged again. Even my strict religious background taught that the answers might be known only after my own death and only if I died in a state of complete grace. There was so much that did not make sense and I did not want to wait until after I died to get answers. As a child I was taught to have trust and faith in God, whom I was raised to believe was a Supreme Being of great love and righteousness but who also had strict judgment and severe punishment for sinners. I had both loved and feared the God I was taught to believe in. Forgiveness by God had to come through confessing sins to a priest who would then be able, by a God given power, to absolve the seriousness of the sins as long as the sinners were sorry for their offenses, promised to sin no more, and would do the prescribed penance. Salvation with entry into heaven was only for the good and worthy. I was sure there must be much more to God and life than the limiting and fear based concepts I had been taught to believe. I had dared to think and question this in my youth. Of course there was no resolution, only reprimand and guilt for questioning the authority of the faith and religious teachings of family, church and school. As I stated earlier those disciplines provided me with a strong foundation, yet now as an adult I felt a responsibility to explore a larger perception of God and life. I had turned to the Bible for answers yet struggled with reading it because it was confusing to me and many passages seemed contradictory and harsh. I instinctively knew there was so much more to learn beyond what had been presented to me thus far. The question was how could I do this and where could I go to gain a deeper understanding and have peace in my soul? It was like standing on a precipice, not really knowing where I was going but definitely knowing I had to go.

For starters, it seemed to me that my expected role as a traditional caring nurse who gave a bed bath, a back rub, the next pain medication or wound treatment was incomplete and one dimensional. Although these measures were important, necessary, and temporarily relieved some or even all of the physical discomfort, there were other types of pain and distress that needed attention. I deeply sensed that the emotional, social, mental and spiritual pain were all connected to the physical distress I witnessed in my patients. What did I really know about these people and their lives before they were sick? What could be the individual non-physical factors contributing to their vulnerability to illness and pain? Since I couldn't know them very personally within the time we had together I sought a common denominator. I realized that everything that applied to them could also apply to me. How well did I really know those factors in my own life? That scared me.

I was the one who was supposed to be in control and help others deal with their feelings. The struggle with my own feelings, questions and inner processes unsettled me. Yet it also provided me with opportunities to learn important and valuable things about myself.

I began to realize that I had areas of inner pain that were nudging me to look at them. Underneath a smile and a pretense that I was fine lurked feelings of old unresolved grief, anger, fear and hurt. Were these all mine? I did have a habit of unwittingly taking on other peoples' pain. My husband called me "the defender of the down and out," always rushing to help anyone and, often unknowingly, relieving them of their own responsibility in the situation. Was I relating much too empathetically with my patients and their circumstances? Was I trying to assuage guilt from my childhood? Was I trying to prove my worthiness? Deep within me was a belief that I was never quite good enough, no matter how much I did or gave or cared. It was a secret place that I tried to hide because it felt shameful. Also, I was very sensitive, a trait that I had learned early in childhood was in many instances considered a weakness or flaw.

My original young and naïve assurance that a traditional structure of nursing would be my life's work was now on shaky ground. I was questioning everything including my own purpose. I began to feel that there was much more to my life's purpose than I could fully grasp. The words holistic and integrative were not part of my nursing vocabulary at that time, nor of anyone else's that

I knew of, yet I understood their meanings. It made sense to me that people lived their lives as interplay between body, mind, emotion, and spirit with the spirit being the essential core of existence and purpose, the all knowing God-like center within each of us. I realized how the spirit is the most powerful part of human beings. Yet that part was often buried below common focus on the physical body. I suspected that many people did not realize this holistic interconnection or believe it because no one, neither personally nor professionally, was able or willing to talk with me about it. Even though these holistic concepts were rational to me I didn't know how to interpret and fully understand them, let alone properly use them to help others. My mind and heart longed to know.

One day an intriguing idea floated into my mind. It was that because of God being our Creator and therefore being within us, we must be co-creators with this Divine Source. That thought felt very valid even though I didn't know the full meaning. Yet at the same time because of my religious background it seemed somehow blasphemous. It would be a few more years before I could truly understand and personally utilize the concept of being a co-creator with God, The Ultimate, Endless, Limitless, Creative Energy Divine Source of All That Is.

During this time there was another mystery going on within me. It was the strong increase of familiar warm and somewhat electric sensations coming through my hands when I reached out to comfort others with a loving and gentle touch. I had been vaguely aware of this feeling as an adolescent. Everyone said my touch and hugs helped soothe and ease their distress. But what were these sensations? I believed that they were coming from a Spiritual Source yet I did not understand the meaning. Often this feeling would magnify in powerful intensity and strength accompanied by a vision and intuitive "knowing" about the person or patient I was attending. It was strange to me and I certainly had no one at that time with whom to discuss this. Whenever I tried to do so I was met with disbelief, dismissal, invalidation or hurtful ridicule. I went to bookstores only to find any information about this at the very back of each store on an isolated corner shelf marked "occult." It was the early 1970's. The sensation I felt was described in these books as spiritual healing energy. I felt odd and uncomfortable hiding in the back of the store to explore this fascinating information, yet felt deeply driven to do so. I was very curious about this energy, why I was feeling it, and how I could learn to medically and holistically utilize it. Despite the bookstore identification as "occult," I trusted all the while that what I felt had to be a good and Divinely inspired spiritual thing because it felt loving, it helped others, and came to me spontaneously.

Since the shocking death of my young patient several years earlier my mind was searching for answers to all of my questions. As my professional nursing and personal life experiences broadened so did my quest for meaning and understanding. A powerful and constant restlessness settled into me and subtly began to interfere with my marriage and home life, although I didn't even recognize that at first. This powerful force stubbornly persisted throughout my many attempts to ignore or dismiss it. The strength of it was also confusing.

Here I was, married to a good man whom I loved, along with our two beautiful, precious and healthy children. I loved my family, cared for our lovely home, enjoyed our pleasant neighborhood, close friends, large family, my chosen nursing career, etc.etc. Why wasn't that enough? Why wasn't I enough? What was this need I had to answer some other calling, to fill some place within me that was crying out to be filled?

I remember often standing at my front door in tears feeling lonely, alone, and wondering what was wrong with me that I could not be fulfilled with what I was doing and with all that I had in my life. I yearned to know more about the energy sensations in my hands, about life, God, pain, suffering, emotions, death, the soul and human spirit, my own hidden self and other purposes for which I was born into this particular life. I felt driven to experience and fulfill those purposes with the proper understanding and commitment. I didn't know if I had the courage and strength to seek and deal with whatever answers I might find. However, there was a constant and ever deepening pull to follow the path of my soul and trust that I would be safely led by Spirit.

My church and many of my family, friends and colleagues advised me to abandon this quest which they all believed was futile, crazy and even dangerous. They could not understand at all. I knew I would be taking a monumental risk by forging ahead and I knew I would be alone in unfamiliar territory. I was failing my parents' expectation of being the good example setter and I was stepping out of the accepted and traditional way of things and the roles I had accepted. I had always done what I was told to do, followed what I was taught and obeyed the rules, even when I disagreed. But now all of that was being greatly challenged by a powerful expansion that was coming from deep within my soul.

I was scared and unprepared for what lay ahead. Yet I absolutely could not, despite how very much I tried, deny the longing of my soul. I had such a desperate need to know and understand my deeper nature. The spiritual pull to continue my search blinded me with its powerful force. I prayed longer and harder. I needed support. I began to see everything in layers as multidimensional and multifaceted with deep meaning and uncommon perspectives. It was like an imprinted inner knowing I could not explain. This made it difficult for me to join others in what were considered typical, expected comments during conversations about news events and social issues. I didn't even know how to explain what I was thinking, feeling, seeing. It was like seeing far beyond an entire forest and at the same time seeing every tree. At one time I was told by a woman I had met who was known as "the mystic" that I was an empath. She explained an empath as someone who is very sensitive and intuitively tuned into the energies and feelings of others and of surrounding circumstances. Wow, this sure sounded like me! Because of this ability I had to learn to distinguish between my own feelings and those of people and activities around me. I also had to learn to protect myself from absorbing into my being what did not belong to me and yet still be effective at helping others. It still was not clear just why all this was happening to me at the time. My prayers were always intertwined with my idealism of expecting the answer to be what I imagined it should be, which was to follow my soul's path while keeping a happy family and intact household. What a humbling awakening I was in for! And so, while I was in this place with myself 40 years ago, a new and undeniable spiritual journey began for me. It was powerfully pulling me forward and my well structured life dramatically changed.

Surprisingly, the first step onto my soul's unfolding path began with a back injury that was serious enough to prevent me from nursing for a few months. After several medical opinions recommending risky surgical procedures I decided to follow my father's advice to see a chiropractor who had successfully treated him a few years earlier. I had not even believed in chiropractic but was desperate to recover without surgical intervention and be able to return to work and properly care for my family and home. At our first meeting that doctor shocked me with his keen ability to see my spiritual struggle even though I had not said anything at all to him about it, nor had my father. As we talked I knew that he understood and respected my longing, my quest, my fears and my many questions about God, life force energy, the interconnection of body, mind, emotion and spirit, and psychic ability. He was very knowledgeable about all of it. It was amazing to me that this doctor lived right in my own town and intuitively knew what I was seeking! During that first appointment he told me that I was a natural channel for healing and needed to learn how to become comfortable and confident utilizing it to help others. It was surely Divine Guidance that led me to meet this special doctor when I did. As he successfully treated my back injury he also directed me to other people who were similarly aware, interested and involved in holistic, spiritual, healing quests and practices. Finally, I had met others with whom to relate! It was such a relief to know I was no longer alone or a strange misfit.

This group of people, some of whom were the doctor's patients, invited me to attend their local meditation meetings. I felt nervous as the new, inexperienced person yet that feeling quickly melted when I was warmly and respectfully welcomed as a "kindred soul." Those in the group taught me the art of meditation, which I had heard was very beneficial to one's entire being. There was a comfortable kinship among those like-minded people who were on a similar journey as I. Learning the many benefits of meditation made me eager to be able to go into deep levels of relaxation and communion with my inner spiritual core. As a girl raised in specific religious doctrine I had been taught the concept and practice of prayer as reciting certain holy words of supplication, praise and gratitude. There was no reference to the idea of meditation. I came to understand that prayer can be highly effective as simply talking to God anytime, anywhere in one's own heartfelt words, and meditation is listening to God's guidance. I was ready to learn more!

Even with all of my good intentions it really was quite challenging to quiet my incessant mind chatter. I was so familiar with the mental activity of praying, that the absence of mental activity needed in meditation was new to me. My mind wandered and demanded that I pay attention to every little thought that loomed large and important in that moment. At first I found it very difficult to let go. I worried I couldn't do it. That resulted in tension and stress, the very things that meditation is intended to relieve. Thankfully, the experienced meditators in the group continually supported and encouraged me. With persistence, regularity and dedication to meditation practice I finally was able to transcend my mind chatter, relax and clearly listen to the still small Voice of Divine inspiration and guidance within me. Well, most of the time, anyway. It did then and continues now to require daily discipline to be still, listen, and hear with clarity to determine the guidance as being from our Creator and not from personal ego.

My new friends also invited me to join them in a series of spiritual/metaphysical classes they had been attending. There they were learning how the body-mind-spirit is interconnected, how to see and interpret the electromagnetic energy fields around the body, often called auras, and how to properly utilize spiritual energy for healing. I was very excited to learn and delighted to be among new like-minded friends. The classes were just what I needed. There were others who shared and understood my quest to know.

I no longer viewed God in the restricted way I was taught in childhood. I began to understand how the Essence of God, as Divine Creative Source Energy, embraces so very much more than I had ever been allowed to know. I was introduced to highly evolved spiritual mentors who taught in depth how we are all intricately, continuously and forever connected to this God Source. It is the true core of our being, our Divine Nature. Our authentic truth is that we are spiritual beings having human experiences. At the end of this book is a clearer explanation of spiritual concepts I came to believe as truth.

During the early phase of my journey my new practice of meditation had provided a window into my own soul's spiritual resourcefulness and co-creative connection with Divine Source. I was no longer afraid to explore my co-creative abilities with God as my ever-present Partner leading the way. I also knew for sure that the strong sensation in my hands was a loving energy of healing that I could consciously and directly channel at anytime from Divine Source through me to others. That allowed me to be able to actually see with my physical eyes and feel with my hands specific energy patterns and auras around people and animals, trees and plants. I could see and feel energy distortions as sources of illness and discomfort. With properly utilizing my spiritual intuition and healing energies I was able to help others regain some measures of calm, comfort, balance, hope and insight which directed a path to whole-person healing.

It all made such good sense to me. I was very excited to share my experiences and understandings and I truly believed that my family would certainly want to hear all about it now. They weren't ready before but surely they would be now.

Since I honestly thought the sharing and demonstration of all this with family and friends was my responsibility, I became quite the enthusiastic proselytizer, always talking about it. However, much to my surprise and dismay, my uninvited, zealously imparted information was not well received. Despite trying different approaches with them, their disinterest and dismissal continued and I soon felt rejected, unappreciated and devalued by everyone close to me. My hurt reaction led to thoughts and behavior that became sprinkled with judgments and self righteousness. How could they think I was being pushy and overbearing? Why couldn't they see me as loving them and just trying to impart new knowledge that would help all of us? I didn't realize then that I really had unfair expectations on them. What I presented to them was very challenging and alien to their ingrained beliefs, models of life, and doctrines of faith. Although they did not really abandon me, they couldn't relate to me. I didn't know how to manage that. I wanted all of us to be happy together. I wanted them to understand and accept me. Maybe they tried to show me that they did and I just couldn't see it then because I was too busy trying to prove that what was right for me was right for them. I needed to learn how such tenacity was my human ego trying to control myself and others. Of course that is neither respectful nor very spiritual.

Before I came to really understand that though, my struggle was long and pervasive and it soon became obvious that I did not and could not fit in my family place anymore. I didn't belong. Conversation was always strained because of my "out of the norm" ideas and opinions. I felt like I was on the outside of a glass house looking at my entire family, friends, and neighbors but not being able to join them inside or get them to join me outside. The glass walls were unbreakable and there were no visible doors. I was very lonely and sad. Although I still felt driven to pursue what I truly believed was my soul's mission, I tried my best several times to be the old me, to forget this inner questing, to properly align again with the expected role functions I had once willingly assumed. Each time I tried to deny this quest I became quite sick with sinus infections, back and stomach problems, injuries, and migraine headaches. I was trying desperately to be true to myself as well as to my family. I knew that I needed to somehow balance my emotional rollercoaster. Having intellectual, physical, and practical understanding of all that I was learning about spirituality, Universal Law, and my soul's multipurpose mission was not enough. I had to surrender to the guidance I was receiving through prayer and meditation. It was then that the next step on my journey catapulted me into deeper levels of my emotional self, the understanding of which I believe is an essential part of anyone's spiritual journey. It is also the most difficult.

It began with my effort to help a very depressed family friend by taking him to an established professional counseling group that had a good success rating. I was allowed to sit in on the first orientation session. That session, much to my surprise, was powerfully insightful for me and resulted in my decision to invest one year in attending semi-monthly group counseling and therapy services offered there. There was only a free will donation requested. I was placed in a selective group for women called "the earth mothers," those known for wanting to take care of the whole world because they felt responsible for everyone. I bristled at being put in that group because I saw nothing wrong with wanting to help everyone. They made it clear that I had a lot to learn about myself. It was true. In that difficult year I was able, despite my frequent resistance, to confront my innermost ambivalent thoughts and feelings, past traumas, defenses, anger, resentment and ego trips that until then I had not even fully admitted to myself. They had been mostly locked up inside me in compartments marked "shame on you" and "not allowed".

The group counseling was very effective. It was amazing to me how unknowingly dishonest one can be with one's own emotions because of fear or shame or guilt. I learned that even though I denied being a victim I was behaving like one and needed to change that. At the outset of this introspection I instinctively knew that this was just the beginning of greater revelations and understandings that I would use to help myself and to eventually help others in a new and deeper way. My soul commitment was reinforced and my spiritual growth was rapidly expanding yet I did not realize at that time the increasing distance and disconnection this would have on my marriage. I honestly thought that as I became more authentic it would improve everything. The idealist dreamer in me was still hopeful.

Deep down I wanted my husband to join me in this venture that I believed was so important. I was certain that if only I could persuade him to at least be interested in conversation about it, we'd be fine, even better as a couple and as a family. He did not deny me following my path yet he personally had no interest and I just had to accept that. The strain on our relationship grew, yet I honestly did not believe that my marriage was really dissolving. I could sense my husband's confusion and rejection of the changes in me. I was not the same "girl" whom he had married 15 years earlier, nor could I be. To him I had become an unrelatable stranger, unable to return to the girl he wanted and with whom he once fell in love. Neither one of us knew how to deal with this. My several attempts to have us go together to counseling failed. Although we remained respectful to each other, our communication became more strained and limited. This of course was causing tension in our children. My adolescent sons were at a vulnerable age and I am sure they were confused and embarrassed that their mother was so different from what was considered the normal, traditional type. Even though we all loved one another and continued our involvements together in the same daily activities, the dynamic of our family was changing. Even while spending several years trying to make it all work I just didn't know how to fix it myself. We were all trying to cope as best we could.

My feeling of isolation and desperation grew over the next two years. Within that time two more events occurred that penetrated my heart with deep pain. My beloved grandmother, who had been a battered woman at the hands of my alcoholic grandfather, suffered a catastrophic stroke. Her only physical ability was to move her eyes, eyes that communicated hopelessness and terror. I spent as much time with her as I could trying to comfort her and ease her distress. She died within a week and I grieved my loss of her while also being thankful that she was free and finally at peace. A short time later a very dear family friend violently ended his own life. There was no warning and the news was shattering. I was asked by his family to be the one to notify people. It was a tremendous burden. I felt engulfed in the sadness of personal losses.

Several months later I was in another town at a spiritual event without my family and I severely injured my back again. This time I was hospitalized and bedfast in traction and treatment for three weeks. Since I had been unable to make a decision about my marriage before this accident, it seemed that my body was forcing me to do so. I literally felt pulled apart in opposite directions. My back injury and pain were representative of the heavy weight I didn't know how to bear. How could I leave the family I loved and yet how could I return to them as the strange and changed person I had become to them and expect them to take care of me, especially now? It would be the same situation as before. I felt I was both a cause of my family's distress as well as a victim of my own inner conflict. Being full of guilt and lonely despair, it was obvious that my husband and I needed to separate. He felt that since I was the one who changed, I should be the one to move out.

We agreed it was best for our adolescent sons to stay with their dad in the home and surroundings familiar and comfortable to them. We agreed to keep our relationship amicable and parent our sons together while in separate houses, with my husband assuming the primary day to day responsibility. I knew how selfish this must have seemed to others, yet I was convinced in my own mind that the separation was temporary. I believed that somehow my husband would agree to go to counseling with me and we'd work it out. Sadly, that was not to happen. The path I felt so driven to follow and the path my husband took would not include us as a couple.

Soon to follow was the judgmental backlash from people in the community. At that time when parents separated or divorced it was highly unusual for children to be left in the primary care of their dad. People did not understand anything that was going on with me so they began to make up stories. Many concluded that the reason I left my sons with their dad was that I was leaving for another man. That was not true. There was even a story of me joining a cult. That was not true either. They did not understand at all. How could they? They had no reference or association to what was really happening with me. I believe that their made-up stories simply made my actions plausible to them.

When I regularly visited with my children and went to their games, school events, and activities, etc., I was polite to those who spoke ill of me. Mostly, the gossipers shunned me. I didn't blame them or expect them to understand or accept me, although it did hurt. I wanted to belong yet I could not. The reality was that I was so torn inside myself that I had to be away to find my center, to express my soul's undeniable, incredibly powerful, unrelenting need to be authentic to the highest spiritual purpose for which I came here. As dramatic as it may sound, this calling went beyond my roles as nurse, wife, mother, family member, and neighbor. It overshadowed my fear and guilt and swept me up in its need to be fulfilled.

I recently re-viewed the movie, "Close Encounters of the Third Kind," and instantly and intimately related with the soul driven energy of Richard Dreyfuss' character. I understood how he could separate from his family with a single mindedness. He instinctively knew he must fulfill his mission even though his family neither understood nor supported it and were hurt, angry, and confused.

It was not his intention to hurt his family. It was never, ever my intention to hurt mine. I've had many times of sadness and grief about this through the years, even though I knew it was my soul's chosen path.

I learned that before being born, we each agree on a spirit-soul level to be in certain relationships and families with each other, often throughout many lifetimes. In these relationships we play roles in each other's lives for healing, balancing, and to help with the higher purpose and deeper understanding of each one's soul mission. I believed that my husband, my sons and myself had all been together before and would be together again in other lifetimes to continue the learning and growth we had determined to do, each separately as well as together. That concept deeply resonated with me in my soul as true, yet in my heart I still felt strong emotions. I prayed for integrity to know for certain that this separation, as part of a soul agreement for each of us, would result in learning and prospering as we were meant to. To my family circle and the friends we had within it, this was a most strange and unbelievable concept. Many thought it was a far- out, convenient excuse to justify my behavior. I had to accept that, knowing that people have their personal opinions and judgments based on their own beliefs, attitudes, perceptions and experiences.

My moving out felt like I had been through a dying experience. Although I sincerely believed it was the best decision for all of us and I stayed actively involved with my children and their dad, I felt a great loss as I believe they did too. It took quite some time for me to deal with all the emotions of such a change as I know it did for them too. I prayed everyday for all of us to know how to adjust, adapt and follow Divine guidance through this.

Muddling through this time of adjustment to being on my own inspired more actively holistic work for me. My understanding and trust of the intricate body-mind-emotion-spirit relationship was expanding. I was very certain that one of my next purposes was to be a hospice nurse to help people more easily and peacefully pass through the last phase of their lives on earth. There is a meaningful process in dying and I wanted to better understand it, both for myself and for the patients and families I would serve. I found an established home hospice service in the area, the only one of its kind then. Despite having only one of the three job requirements, I was told that I was hired based on my enthusiasm, sincerity and desire, all of which came through in a heart-felt letter I had written to the director. The environment of helping people in their dying processes in their own homes was a real catalyst to further developing and sharing my holistic work. As I learned about my own life's value I was simultaneously able to help my patients learn to focus on the value of actively living as honestly and as best they could in whatever time they had left. For myself, I was learning to regard each moment as precious and alive with creativity and I was able to teach them to do so even as they approached death. In turn, they helped me to face my personal issues with more courage and strength. I can still vividly recall certain patients with their significantly inspiring situations and my profound interactions with them. Three of the most meaningful and special ones are recounted in other chapters of this book.

After five years of my beloved hospice nursing in a very supportive environment, the hospice facility was forced to close due to underfunding. That was a sad loss for me. There was no other area hospice at that time. Being hopeful that I could continue my holistic philosophy of nursing elsewhere with all my experience, I returned to hospital nursing as a "float" to go to wherever I was needed. I tried to be sent as often as possible to departments with patients who were considered terminal. However, my holistic style while appreciated by patients and their families, was not readily accepted by staff in those facilities as it had been at hospice. Some of the hospital physicians and supervisors were especially unsupportive about this "whole person" concept in which they had no real understanding. I have several stories about situations for which I was reprimanded for going outside of the acceptable nursing role in those early days. I'll relate just one of them here.

Once when I was making patient rounds on the midnight shift I found a patient awake and quite upset. He was scheduled to have triple bypass heart surgery at 8 am, which meant he would be prepared at 7 a.m. It was then 2 a.m. and he still had not slept despite already being given two doses of the ordered sedative. Since every other patient was asleep I was free to spend time listening to his fears and concerns, offering him support, showing him how to do deep breathing and relaxation exercises. I massaged his tense neck and back muscles and administered energy healing to him. He repeatedly voiced his gratitude as he fell asleep with a relaxed face and body. Before my shift was over he went into surgery with calm and confidence. The operation was successful and I later learned that he healed more quickly and easily than the doctors expected. However, I was called into the supervisor's office the following night and reprimanded for ignoring protocol which was to just give the patient another dose of medication and call the chaplain. She said I should not have spent all that time myself with an upset patient away from the nurses' station. That same station was manned by three other nurses who knew where I was and could easily do the hourly checks on other patients without me. It was a very quiet night so there was no good reason for me to be anywhere else. The supervisor neither valued nor understood my holistic care to the patient, even though it was very effective for his relief from stress. It was 22 years later that I had the wonderful opportunity to be hired by a progressive hospital as the integrative therapy nurse whose job was to minister to patients in exactly this way, holistically and with healing energy.

A few years after the story of my patient with heart surgery I once again severely injured my back while lifting a paralyzed patient. The injury made me unable to return to that type of nursing service. In questioning why this happened I realized that each back injury had occurred at a time when I felt a lack of support. The body has an amazing way of sending us messages to pay attention to our thoughts and emotions and deviations from our spiritual path. While healing from this newest injury I was inspired with additional life purpose. The familiar warm and energized sensations in my hands that I had long ago learned to utilize as a comforting, healing touch energy was now stronger than ever. It had been very helpful to my hospital and hospice patients and now I knew it was time to again utilize it for my own healing efforts as well as to teach others about it. It was now mid to late 1980's and there was some interest from a few curious colleagues in learning about my philosophy and healing modalities.

After recovering from the back injury, I offered to teach an 8 week course in meditation and relaxation at the local college. My offer was denied because the college had never before had such a class and thought it would not attract the community. Not being easily daunted, I tried again and though I received much skepticism from administration, I was allowed an interview by the college Dean. It was a rather comical interview. As I entered his office, I thought I had stepped into another time period. The room was very messy, chock full of book and paper clutter and dimly lit with dusty, dark and heavy curtains. The professor had long gray hair and beard, was dressed in a rumpled tweed jacket, held a pipe in his mouth while looking sternly at me through small round glasses settled on the edge of his nose. He held onto my resume while he walked all around me, looking me up and down. I felt uncomfortable and ready to tell him so until he said with a soft voice and genuine smile, "Well, Jean Daly, you don't look crazy to me, so I'll give you a chance with this unconventional idea of yours. Get in your curriculum for approval and we'll see how it is. But you must get at least 8 people for the class or we will have to cancel it."

I was delighted. Of course I had not yet written the course but I had no doubt it would be a motivating, exciting undertaking for me. Upon acceptance of my submission the 16 hour course was advertised by the college. To everyone's surprise including mine, the class was overfilled with 20 students, the maximum capacity for the available room, as well as a long waiting list. By the end of the first 2 hour class, students were asking me for my business cards which of course were nonexistent at that point. I quickly created them for the next class. They also asked me for private counseling and healing sessions and many more classes. I was astonished at the receptivity. Their interest and support eventually led me to a full time private practice as a holistic therapist, counselor and educator. My clients ranged in age from 5 to 83 years, presenting with many and varied disorders. It was multifaceted healing work that people who came to me were hungry for and ready to experience. This work was very effective and felt so right in my soul that my practice quickly expanded, with no need for advertisement, and lasted for very many years even through semi-retirement. The college supported me in developing many additional holistic healing and metaphysical courses. I taught there each semester for 15 years. My son called me a pioneer in these ventures. I thought about submitting articles on my work to professional publications yet I convinced myself that I was too busy then to write about my journey. More truthfully though, I was just not ready. Despite the success of my healing, teaching and counseling work beginning in the 1980's, it would be many more years before holistic philosophy and healing techniques would be generally accepted and become mainstream in our culture and in medicine. Today they are being taught in many nursing schools.

Throughout my experiences I could feel much Divine support and guidance, strength and courage to continue this path. Whenever possible I traveled across the country to learn new techniques from professional masters in esoteric healing and in transpersonal, holistic counseling. I incorporated these into my work and teachings as well as into my personal growth and development.

Over the years my additional studies resulted in several more professional certifications which added to my credentials. Some of these were The One Brain Integration System, Imago Relationship Therapy for couples, singles, and families, Mastership Level in Reiki Energy Healing, Loss and Grief counseling, Interactive Guided Imagery, Creative Visualization, Puberty and Adolescent programs, Women's Health seminars and workshops. I also studied body/mind counseling techniques for groups, prosperity consciousness, acupressure, the use of crystal energy, herbal and flower remedies, tai chi, yoga and ayurvedic medicine. All of these interventions were rewarding to me to know that my proper utilization of them created healing effects on all levels of a person's being.

During the same time as my private client practice and my career of teaching classes for continuing education at the college, I also taught in various professional, hospital, and community venues. I led a weekly meditation group in my home and at one time there were two groups. I had successfully created more than 20 integrative healing and self development programs that people said were very helpful to them. Quite a few people, including young people, have told me verbally and in letters that my interactive holistic counseling with them literally saved their lives. That deeply touched my heart. I feel very humbled by this and by the numerous inspirational stories from people recounting to me how what I presented made a positive difference in their lives in many ways. This was reciprocal because I always learned much from my students and clients too. Gratitude flowed between us. To this day I still hear from several of my very special clients. I am especially proud of the ones I counseled as children who are now grown. They tell me of their happy lives and families. These are privileges for which I shall always be truly grateful.

Beginning in the early fall of 1988 there was a 9 month interruption of my work with others when I was recovering from a serious illness during which I had a vivid near death experience. This is known as an NDE and is recounted in another chapter of this book. Now all these years later I can relive that experience with the same emotional intensity that I felt during that incredible out of body experience. The immense peace, the all encompassing love and light were truly and totally amazing. Because of that phenomenal experience I know for certain that the 12 year old girl who died in my arms so many years earlier went peacefully and easily to a place of astounding light and joy. I actually saw her and was able to completely let go of the guilt I had felt over her death. Also, I have no fear at all of death for I absolutely know it is not an end to life but merely a transition to the living spirit form of continued existence in the presence of the Creator.

My learning deepened after my NDE. I came to trust even more that there is an order in the Universe despite the appearance of chaos. I understood more completely that I am not in control of everything, yet I am responsible for my thoughts, feelings, behaviors and self-discipline at all times, thereby creating my own reality in many ways. This is true for each of us. I came to more fully trust that, no matter what, I am infinitely and in every moment loved by God, the Divine Source Essence who is always and ever available to me and to each of us with totally unconditional love.

Yet even now, as new situations, decisions and old memories arise, I can feel my human self struggle. At those times I need to give honest, full and safe expression physically, verbally, or in journaling, to all of my emotions and feelings when I am alone. Afterward, I can utilize holistic techniques to become more centered, to return to the truth I know and be open to fresh perspectives and understandings. I deeply value the effective healing techniques I have learned and taught which I continue to share with others who are willing to learn. Among them are techniques from the courses of study I had previously listed as well as several others I have since learned. Now in this present time it is so much easier to research the readily available volumes of information on body-mind-spirit interactions, the nature of spirituality and laws of the Universe. This information includes all forms of integrative healing techniques, such as Reiki, videos of auras and energy fields around the body, and the Chakra system which is comprised of active energy centers that correspond to the physical endocrine system. There is a wealth of valuable material from which to learn and understand the fascinating complexity of ourselves. I urge you, my readers, to research wisely from reputable sources, and always with the most reverent, positive, loving intentions. Over the years of my journey I've had personal visits and discussions with wonderful fellow travelers and teachers. Among them are Louise Hay, Wayne Dyer, Deepak Chopra, Neale Donald Walsch, and Mike Dooley. My time with each of them was very enriching to my spiritual growth.

Even so, all these years later it still can sadden me that my marriage did not survive. We did not have the skills then to know how to handle it all. The changes in our family and in our sons' daily lives were difficult adjustments, yet they provided opportunities for all of us to grow and evolve. My husband and I eventually divorced. We made it uncontested and respectful through a mediator and we remained friends, which our sons always appreciated. Throughout my soul's journey I had to learn how to truly accept all of myself and others and am continuing to work at it. I also had to learn how to forgive myself and others, as well as to ask for and receive their forgiveness. Now in this later stage of my life I sometimes still reflect on how I could have done it all differently. Even with the wisdom I've gained through my long journey I still do not know, given that particular time period and my personal background. I recently heard someone say that forgiveness is giving up the hope that the past could be any different. Yet, I honestly believed then as I do now that in being true to my own spirit-soul mission I could better understand myself and more authentically serve and care for my family, albeit in a different way. I believe we each need to find and accept our own authentic soul self. As any one of my cherished family walk their own path and might ask for my assistance I would gladly help them. I'd offer them gentle whispers of encouragement from the sidelines with unconditional love, light and support. Hopefully their journeys are easier for them.

I am grateful and happy to be more easily and comfortably connected to all of my family now. Many years ago my beloved parents returned to their spiritual home and I am thankful that while they were still with me here, we were able to gain a deeper love, understanding and acceptance. As for my sons, considering the difficult adjustments they had to make in their adolescence, I am most especially proud of the very fine wonderful men they have grown up to be. I could not love them more. My sons and their families as well as my siblings, all accept that I definitely "march to the beat of a different drummer." In my older age now, although still full of passion, ideas and ideals, I am less serious-minded, more relaxed, and more lighthearted and spontaneous. It delights how often people tell me I am funny and fun! That's a good feeling. It's freeing to be less serious! Spending time with all of my large family, especially my three wonderful teenage grandchildren is enjoyable and particularly extra special to me. We can all have fun, laugh and play, even tease and give voice to dissenting opinions and beliefs, while being assured that we each love and cherish one another.

With any new challenge presented to me by a family member, friend, student or client, with every training, every directional change, every additional purpose, every set back, I learn, stretch and grow, wait and trust, and move toward being more gracefully authentic. At times I still stumble and fall on my way. I'm grateful to know how to pick myself up and connect again with God Source for guidance. My faith continues to be my strongest support. With faith and my willingness to follow my purpose as Spirit directs, I can continue to make meaningful and helpful contributions to the lives of others. My own acronym for the word CARE is:

C- compassionate A- authentic R- respectful
E- empowering.

For many years and to the present time my inner work has continued in different settings and structures. There have been struggles and uncertainties along the way, to be sure, and these were my teachers too. For as much as I have discovered, learned, experienced, understood, and shared with others, I am still amazed at how much more there is to learn and understand. We each have a special purpose here with opportunities to make a positive difference in this world with a legacy of love and kindness. These are life's truest healers. I know I will always continue to learn and grow, even after my death. My belief is that life continues in a conscious spirit form. During my own near death experience I was witness to that profound reality. It is there that we totally understand the eternal presence and value of Divine Unconditional Love. It's not yet my time to leave this life so it's my responsibility to keep going forward, knowing that the Essence of God is always within me as guidance and around me as reflection. I believe this is true for each person. We need to pay close attention to that still small Voice, that gentle Whisper within that is our most accurate guidance.

As I re-live and share the following stories of my experiences, I am deeply grateful for this amazing soulful journey. And so it continues, day by day and beyond........

A Conditional Challenge from Dad

During the early days of my experiences in channeling healing energy, my parents had no understanding, acceptance or belief in what I was doing. They did honor and respect my ability to provide comfort, soothing, help and hope to others within my roles as a good Christian, a family member and a nurse. However, within my strict religious upbringing any hands on healing treatment was reserved for a special few of God's devout chosen ones, usually a saint or extra holy religious person or privileged priest. For the rest of us to be doing this was considered a supernatural, occult action that was sacrilegious.

My parents felt that they needed to protect me from what they considered to be against the Church's teachings. Therefore, they were not supportive of my desire and efforts to learn more about energy healing and the metaphysical concepts that I have described within this book.

I knew in my soul that even though I was not a special holy person, this restriction did not apply to me. I was certain that the sensation of energy I had felt coming through my hands since childhood was from God and was channeled through me to be positively purposeful. I truly believed I had a responsibility to properly learn how to utilize it to help others. Mom, being a very staunch Catholic, was especially concerned about my pursuit. It was taking me beyond the limits of a system in which I had been raised. Dad, even while standing with Mom's disapproval, had a curiosity. Dad had always been interested in science fiction, the possibility of other inhabited worlds and dimensions beyond our normal everyday consciousness. However he did not pursue this interest outside of reading and the frequent viewing of his favorite old movie, "The Forbidden Planet." On his practical side as a police detective he decided to investigate what his daughter was involved in.

One day during a visit with my parents the conversation about what I was doing was peppered with their usual protesting comments. However, that day there was a surprising twist. My Dad suddenly challenged me to "prove that this healing stuff is real." For many years he had suffered with the painful, scaly, itchy rash of psoriasis on his forearm. He regularly applied the only available prescribed medication with little to no relief of the severe rash. During that particular visit my dad wanted, actually dared me, to cure his psoriasis with healing energy. His challenge came with the condition that if it really cured his rash he would be willing to accept my work and even be interested in learning more about it.

I explained to him that healing could not be demanded and that it did not always result in a cure as he meant it. One could not demand that the result be a certain way in a certain time frame to prove it was valid. Also, if one's specific expectations were not met, that did not mean that the healing energy had failed or was bogus.

I further explained to Dad how healing energy is never wasted. It goes holistically to wherever the person most needs it. Our inner wisdom continually seeks ways to maintain health and harmony throughout body, mind, emotion and spirit. Unresolved issues in mind, emotion or spirit can manifest in the body as dis-ease, a precursor to actual disease. For example, while a skin rash or infection may be the result of an injury or systemic illness, genetics or allergic reaction to a substance, it also can have its source in an emotional issue. When that issue remains unresolved and is "getting under the person's skin." it can manifest as a rash. Or it can be the body's way of showing that a person is "itching" to accomplish or complete something that has had frustrating delays. Or it can mean that this is the body's way of reacting to stress, anxiety and worry. In all these cases the healing energy would need to go first to that emotional source. The energy would enable the person to have the inspiration of new thoughts and ideas, strength and understanding needed to resolve the issue. Once resolved there would no longer be a need for the skin irritation that came to the surface as a physical manifestation of the underlying discontent. When a person has discovered and resolved the issue that created disharmony in mind, emotion or spirit, harmony can be restored throughout their being. The physical representation of that issue no longer needs to exist in the body, thus, dis-ease doesn't become disease.

It is not a healing channel's place to judge or try to figure out what the issue is for the person. Although oftentimes during the channeling I would receive intuitive information to relate to the client for them to consider. This was not to be judged by me. The channel's service lies in his or her ability to clear a path for the client to receive the healing and choose to accept its flow. I told my dad all these things. He had a hard time relating to the idea of a skin condition having anything to do with an emotional issue. He dismissed that notion and still insisted on setting the challenge. So I began as I always have, still do and always will, with humility, sacred intention and the focused preparedness to channeling healing energy.

I explained to my detective father how a typical session with a patient or client begins. First, I request their permission as they become comfortable in a seated or lying position. I become quiet and still, breathe deeply and slowly, set my intention to be of service, prayerfully center myself in alignment with God's Divine Will and invite my team of spiritual helpers to assist both me and my client. The next step is to affirm to my clients that they are protected, safe and loved. I ask them to become physically comfortable while remaining fully clothed, to close their eyes, to breathe long slow breaths, to clear their mind, and relax. With the client's agreement I play soft beautiful music or soothing sounds to support relaxation. Often I do an energy scan by slowly moving my hands over the body, a few inches away from it. This enables me to feel the electromagnetic energy field, which is a blueprint of the physical, to determine areas of distortion, imbalance, congestion or depletion. Then I gently place my hands on the client either directly or just above the body, depending on the client's comfort level.

The energy healing easily flows through me and becomes stronger throughout the session as I am intuitively guided to direct it in the most appropriate ways for that person. The client may feel one, some, or all of the following; warmth, tingling, a pleasant fullness, sense of gentle pressure, deep relaxation, comfort and well-being. A person may fall asleep. At times, a client may feel no sensation other than relaxation. At times someone may feel a temporary increase in discomfort. This is usually due to long held or deep disharmony within the system that needs to be lifted to the surface to be cleared out so it can be healed. A metaphor to explain this would be one of an old closed wound with a festering infection under the skin. The opening of skin and cleansing of infection would cause more discomfort temporarily until it was cleared so that the real healing can take place.

My dad acknowledged that he understood yet I must say that he was not very cooperative with all my normal preparations. He chose to sit upright in a straight chair with open eyes while trying to direct the process, telling me he wanted this to be done in a short time frame. With this kind of resistance I knew I needed extra angels around us both! Eventually he agreed to close his eyes and made efforts to slow and deepen his breathing.

I began the healing session and despite Dad's initial impatience, he followed my whispered reminders to keep breathing slowly which then allowed him to relax and more easily receive. The flow of energy continued until I felt it begin to dissipate, the signal that he had absorbed all that was needed for that time. I told him it was completed for now. As Dad opened his eyes he looked at the area of psoriasis which was still present and frowned. He had an "I told you so" look, yet thanked me for trying. Although he said he felt some minor relief then, he was sure the healing had not been effective in any major way, reinforcing what he already believed. I explained to my dad that I was always available to him to channel again. Actually, it would have really surprised me if he ever asked for another channeling. I hugged him with love and appreciation for being willing to receive the session, said goodnight, and left for home.

The next day my dad called me to say that when he awoke in the morning he was totally shocked to see the psoriasis on his forearm completely gone! He excitedly described the skin as clear, renewed, soft, pink, comfortable, and there was no scarring. Considering my dad's skeptical and challenging attitude I was pleasantly surprised to hear about such a dramatic result! As soon as I could visit him again I saw for myself that there was indeed a complete healing, a cure of my father's severe skin condition. Of course we were both very grateful for this powerful outcome. Now he was ready to accept my work and intrigued to learn and receive more.

I learned that it is not necessary for a person to consciously believe in the healing of Divine Energy in order for it to be effective. At the core of our being is the Universal Truth that we are spiritual beings having a human experience. From that inner soul place of absolute knowingness, we are in alignment with all possibility and creativity. We can actually experience in the physical world what some may call a miracle. I believe that my dad and I agreed on that soul level, beyond the conscious mind, to share in that healing cure so that he could further explore his own desire to really know, trust and believe.

This story has another surprising twist. Sometime after my session with Dad, there was a party at which he was being honored. All of the family was in attendance and Dad was proud to introduce each of us individually. When he came to me he introduced me as his eldest child and first daughter. Then he said something I couldn't believe I was hearing. He told everyone there that I was a healer and that I had cured his psoriasis. He pulled up his sleeve to show his clear, smooth skin. He also told them that I could see and feel auras and energy fields. He volunteered me to see and describe someone's aura and to demonstrate healing so they could see for themselves. I was dumbstruck! It was obvious by my dad's enthusiastic voice and smile that he was proud and wanted to show his support of me. While I was very glad about that, I had to graciously decline. It was not the time nor the place nor the appropriate situation for me to accept my father's well meaning invitation. I felt like I'd be performing. It was his party, his time to shine, and I'd be distracting from the attention he rightly deserved that night. As I whispered all this to my dad he realized he had inadvertently put me on the spot. He then humorously told everyone my healing sessions needed a quiet place and they were all too noisy. Dad had a great knack for using humor to deflect an awkward moment.

It was a very special gift to me to have my father's acceptance and blessing. I am so grateful that we had that healing experience together. Not only did my dad remain free of the psoriasis, he was more trusting of the process of spiritual healing energy. There was also another blessing. While my mother had been delighted for her husband's healing she was confused by how to incorporate that into her own belief system. It was years later that Mom was able to expand her consciousness to allow acceptance of her daughter's ability and responsibility to utilize spiritual energy for healing. She became more open to understanding that this was my soul's path. Her eventual acceptance was especially heartwarming for me. She saw that the faith in which she had raised me was appreciated and respected by me. It had served as an important and strong foundation for my broadening understanding of spirituality and my soul's mission here. I was so happy to be finally able to share this comfortably with Mom. I wish we would have had more time together. The last time I saw my mother she and Dad were visiting me. We had such an enjoyable time together that weekend, yet I saw that Mom was very tired. She had recently completed rehabilitation after her heart surgery and was very frustrated that she had to moderate her activities. She really disliked that and disliked how quickly she tired. Mom resisted the need to slow down. To comfort her I offered Reiki healing and was delighted that she accepted a full session. Mom was able to truly relax and actually enjoy the feeling of deep rest. I think that was a first for her! She slept soundly that night and seemed to have a lightness about her as she awoke. When my parents were leaving my home later that day I suddenly had an extremely powerful urge to have a photo taken of Mom and me together. Although they were getting into the car at that moment, it could not wait until another time. It had to be right then. My dear dad complied and I shall always be grateful to him for that. It was 10 days later that my beautiful mother died. Our last photo together was gracefully framed in soft pastels by a loving client of mine as a gift to me. It is a treasure. Mom's pretty smile with me beside her, arm in arm, forever adorns my wall.

I miss my beloved parents who have both been gone from this life for years now. I am certain they are enjoying exceptional happiness together in their spiritual home. I am just as certain they now fully understand me and support that which I aspire to positively contribute to the world. I feel their unconditional love, guidance and inspiration for me and for all our family. I know I speak for all of us as I say, "Thank you, thank you very much, Dad and Mom."

Stories of Hospice

The following poem, copied here with the authors' permission, is a prelude to the following heartwarming stories of three very special patients I had the privilege of serving as their hospice nurse. This poem, which I have shared many times in presentations to others about hospice care, has always inspired me. It is my pleasure to share it here with gratitude to its authors.

<u>Poem by</u>
<u>Karen Kauffman Knibbe, RN,</u>
<u>(Karen S. Kauffman, PhD. CRNP, RN, FAAN)</u>
<u>and Robert Buckingham, III, Ph.D.</u>

TEACH ME TO DIE AND I'LL TEACH YOU TO LIVE

Teach me to die, hold out your hand

There are so many things I don't understand

Teach me to die, let me stay home

I've never felt so much alone

Teach me to die as you give of yourself

My life is soon finished, yours still full of wealth

Teach me to die, show me you care

Is it so hard? Won't you take my dare?

Teach me to die, talk of your sorrow

I have time now, maybe none tomorrow

Teach me to die, don't hide your tears

Show me you love me, allay my worst fears

Teach me to die, help ease my pain

I've only my life to lose yet still so much to gain

Teach me to die, help me find peace

We've so much to share and I soon will cease

Teach me to die, I've still much to give

You teach me to die and I'll teach you to live.

Trudy's Transformation

In 1982 I had just begun my new job as hospice nurse, a position for which I had eagerly applied. Although I fulfilled only one of the three application requirements I was told that the job position was granted to me because of my sincere and enthusiastic letter. The letter I wrote to accompany my application revealed my strong heartfelt desire to care for hospice patients and their families in their own homes. This position allowed me to care for a person as a whole being, interconnected in body, mind, emotion, and spirit, which was and always will be the holistic concept so ingrained in my nature. I was thrilled to be hired and could hardly wait to begin.

My very first patient was a woman named Trudy. Her doctor and family had set up hospice care for her because she was suffering from terminal and metastasized lung cancer and needed special help to ease her end of life distress. I was eager to meet her and begin my new role as her hospice nurse.

On my first in-home visit to Trudy I encountered an angry, resentful, demanding woman who knew she was dying and intensely hated everything about her dire situation. She was confined to a hospital bed in her living room, suffering from much pain and discomfort, unable to care for her own basic needs. Trudy clearly stated that she did not want me there. In fact she ordered me to get out of her house. Her daytime care-giver whispered to me that I was surely going to have my hands full and that she herself felt unwelcomed there. However Trudy, having resigned herself to the fact that she had to depend on someone for her personal care needs, begrudgingly allowed the nurse's aide to stay. My own role there was that of assessing Trudy's vital signs and medical needs, providing pain relief and comfort measures as well as giving her emotional support. All of this was within a holistic plan I would create for Trudy personally, in an effort to make her dying process as gentle and comfortable as possible. My care would also extend to her family members who were her two adult daughters, both of whom lived in their own homes.

I knew my first task was to gain Trudy's trust in me. She, like most dying patients, felt extremely vulnerable and struggled with the harsh fear of losing all control. Displays of anger are often the outward expressions that mask deep inner fear, hurt, grief and sadness. I had to respect where Trudy was in her process, especially on that first day, so I immediately acknowledged, accepted, and validated her anger. I told her of my intentions to do all I could to ease her pain and discomfort and then I would leave. After some strong resistance she finally allowed me to medicate her. I told her I needed to return to assess the pain relief effect. She was still quite angry so I gave her some of the control she desperately needed by inviting her to set the time of my next visit. My offer seemed to calm her a bit and she reluctantly agreed to have me see her once again but said she didn't want me there on any regular basis. As I left that first day her tone seemed to be slightly softer and I felt encouraged that my next visit would be better received.

When I returned for the second visit Trudy was throwing things on the floor and refusing to eat. Her voice had a raspy forced strength as she angrily chastised the aide for some small infraction of harsh demands Trudy had placed on her. My arrival at that time made matters worse and I was again firmly told by an irate Trudy to leave the house along with the aide. Her eruption of fiery anger, although very real and valid in itself, also masked much fear, hurt and pain. I knew I had to take the lead and somehow remedy this intense situation, but the nervousness inside me was pretty uncomfortable. I wasn't sure exactly how to handle it all. Here was my very first hospice patient vehemently refusing, even more than she had the previous day, my effort to help her. Before attempting to calm my patient I first needed to calm myself and give comforting reassurance to Trudy's upset aide who was close to tears.

We sat together in another room. Beginning with long, slow deep breathing to release my own anxiety I prayed for guidance and inspiration and mentally visualized all three of us enveloped in soft, calming pink light. I had experience working with the healing vibrations of colors and soft pink was most effective in supporting a sense of relaxation, calm and comfort. After directing the aide to continue her slow deep breathing while visualizing pink light, I gathered my strength and confidence, went out to Trudy and boldly sat next to her. My intention was to convince her that I could quietly listen with support and understanding to her expressions of honest thoughts and feelings in whatever way she needed to do so. At first she resisted yet did not actually refuse. That was encouraging. As I imagined waves of pink light flowing into and around Trudy, her resistance began to weaken. She admitted doubting that what she might say would really matter to anyone. I assured her it did indeed matter to me and to others who cared about her and told her she could begin with giving herself permission. My patient needed all the time and encouragement I could give her and when she was ready to allow herself to start trusting that she would be heard without judgment, she slowly began to reveal her story.

I learned that although much of Trudy's rage was directed toward her disease and the way it had ravaged her body, incapacitated her, and robbed her of her independence, her deepest anger and pain were due to the sudden and recent deaths of her beloved husband and young adult son within a year of each other. The tragic death of her son had happened just six months earlier. Trudy felt helpless to cope with her intense grief and she felt hopeless about her own recently diagnosed terminal illness. She verbalized to me her two simultaneous and conflicting desires. One was to end all the agony and die quickly. The other was to be cured or to live in remission to honor her husband's and son's lives with more meaning and to be there for her two adult daughters. Trudy also was very angry at God but because she had been raised as a good Christian woman who should never question God, she felt very conflicted and guilty about this. She was uncertain what she believed about life after death so this too scared her.

I was keenly aware that Trudy's venting was a crucial step in her process and I gave her all the space she needed to express her emotional pain. Nurses need to be attentive, non-judgmental listeners and maintain sincere compassion while at the same time keeping their own emotional reactions in check. However, in home hospice care there is a unique bond that forms between nurse and patient that can transcend that emotional boundary. This happened to me as I listened to Trudy's outpouring of pain and fear. My compassion blended with admiration for Trudy's bravery and I found my own heart and hand often reaching out to touch hers with love and comfort as tears misted my own eyes.

Trudy continued speaking and sobbing until she felt exhausted with enough inner release to allow her to lie back to rest. What a gift of courage and strength she had given herself! I believe Trudy's willingness to share her story resulted in her first real ability to trust me. At the end of that second visit she asked me to come back to be her nurse. For the next 4 months I regularly visited Trudy nearly every day and witnessed the steady unfolding of her wondrous transformation.

One day early in our relationship Trudy was having severe pain in her chest and her increased anxiety seemed to delay any relief from medication she had received. I asked her to allow me to gently place my hands over her chest as a comfort measure. She agreed and as I lightly placed my hands on her I opened myself as a channel of healing energy for her easement and comfort. In an instant the familiar warmth of the energy that I had learned years earlier how to channel from God Source through myself to others began to flow. I encouraged Trudy to breathe slowly and to think of something pleasing and calming. She chose a favorite scene of being on a lovely beach gazing out at clear, calm, turquoise water. I gave her simple, positive affirmations to repeat in her mind as she visualized herself relaxing on the beach and imagining each ocean wave gently coming in, spraying her with peace and comfort and each wave going out, taking away her pain and distress. Helping Trudy to center on that scene and keep her breathing even and relaxed became my single focus. The combination of Trudy's willingness to mentally participate and the warm flow of healing energy proved effective for her gradual relaxation and relief from pain. Trudy told me she was grateful for this result although she did not understand how it all happened. She was tired then so we agreed to talk about it another day.

When I arrived for the next visit Trudy was again uncomfortable and restless. She asked me to "do that thing again." This time I had brought along a small tape recorder to play soothing music with a background of ocean waves as I placed my hands over her. We began the relaxation session with Trudy following my guidance to breathe, relax her body and settle into a mental visualization of her peaceful place on the beach. I began my own prayer of intention and gratitude for Divine guidance and assistance to center me and lead the way. The energy in my hands quickly grew strong and my patient became more relaxed. This time Trudy commented on the feeling of warm, calming sensations in her chest. Her discomfort was dissolving and she fell asleep. When she awoke Trudy asked me what I was doing with my hands that helped her feel more comfortable. And so began the first of our many conversations about the modalities I was sharing with her; channeling of healing energy from the Divine Source that is God, the connection of mind, body, emotion and spirit, the meaningful art of visualization, and the power of relaxation and meditation. Each time I visited Trudy we included this energy healing and relaxation session as an important and valued part of her standard medical hospice care. She expressed how much she looked forward to it. The nurse's aide even commented on Trudy's attitude change and how glad she was for it since she could care more easily and more completely for her patient. Trudy also began requiring less pain medication. That was a rewarding surprise.

Right from the start I made sure that Trudy understood that the word healing meant "to make whole". That did not promise a cure although for some it might result in a cure. An authentic definition of healing is an intended process of re-integrating every aspect of a person's entire being which involves body, mind, emotions, and spirit, into the natural state of balanced, smooth, rhythmic and harmonious flow of energy and wholeness. This natural state, present in each person, is our true innate spiritual heritage, direct from our Creator.

For most people a physical disease process begins with a dis-ease, which means a fragmentation or disconnection in one or several of the parts of their being. Left unattended and unhealed it eventually becomes a disease. Understanding this concept became a goal for Trudy and is in fact a necessary and important understanding in every person's daily life as well as in one's dying process. In life and in death we can be at ease when all of the aspects of our being are in balance and harmony. Achieving and maintaining this orderliness requires a willingness to make daily conscious efforts to become attuned to the thoughts, emotions, stressors, attitudes, and beliefs, which can have a disruptive impact on the body. It is with that information about ourselves that we can make appropriate and necessary changes which can then lead to balanced integration, easement, healing and wholeness. This is true for everyone, even as a person may be dying.

Throughout the 4 month time period of my hospice nursing care to Trudy her attitude dramatically changed from how I had first encountered her as an angry, frightened woman. Now her focus was on accepting her dying process in the most peaceful and loving manner possible. She was more comfortable in several ways. Her physical pain and discomfort were under control. She was able to talk freely about her struggles with fear and grief and guilt. She was able to relax and be soothed. Trudy asked many questions about end of life preparations and acceptance. She initiated conversations about God, spiritual themes, the importance of forgiveness of herself and others, the actual moment of death, and her uncertain thoughts about going to the place called heaven. She was not sure she was deserving or even that such a place was real for her. The depth of our continuing conversations was fascinating. I truly came to know so much about the heart and soul of this very special woman.

As she drew closer to the end of her life Trudy became interested in sorting through her possessions and giving each one a new home, be it to a relative or a friend or a charity. She insisted on giving me a beautiful multi-colored jacket which I wore with great fondness for many years. Trudy's two daughters were relieved to see the improvements in their mother's attitude and demeanor and felt able to talk and relate more easily with her. This mother and her daughters were healing their previously strained relationships. A renewed trust, easement, and comfort was unfolding in the relationship between them. They began to share poignant family stories, funny memories and lovely sentiments of gratitude, caring and love. Witnessing all of these positive reflections of healing and transformation was indeed an inspiring and special experience to behold.

One day Trudy received a call from her church pastor and she told him of the healing work we were doing together and of her renewed relationship with God. He seemed quite intrigued especially since Trudy had avoided interaction with him and the church after her diagnosis. The pastor was excited to learn of Trudy's active participation in this healing and asked to speak with me about it. Our conversation evolved into the formation of a renewed support system for Trudy from the pastor and church members as well as an invitation for me to speak to them about the spirit-mind-body connection. It would not be until after Trudy's funeral that I would actually speak to her church congregation about this concept and about my evolution of experiences with this beautiful and brave woman. It was my honor to do so. When I did tell my story of Trudy's transformation to her church congregation, there were quite a few members who told me that they felt inspired and ready to integrate the concepts of holistic healing into their lives. They felt that becoming more personally active and holistically responsible for themselves would deepen their faith in partnership with God and expand their overall wholeness. I know Trudy would have joined me in being so pleased about that.

During the last weeks of Trudy's life she told me that she began seeing "glimpses of heaven." She related seeing some of her deceased relatives and friends smiling at her from a beautiful place of light, a light that shone through them to make them appear as glowing spirit forms, yet recognizable to her. I knew when Trudy was experiencing these visions. Her face became very serene and soft, almost translucent. She often nodded, smiling with her lips gently moving as if replying to private messages she was receiving. For me these were sacred times that I was privileged to witness.

As much as Trudy enjoyed these glimpses and was comforted by them she was troubled by the fact that she did not see her husband or her son. Trudy knew her days on earth were quickly coming to an end and she longed to know that she would see her husband and son. She asked everyday for them to come and yet they did not appear.

It was a Tuesday afternoon when Trudy had a particularly long and pleasant reverie. Her face was more translucent and more peaceful than I had ever seen before. Her breathing was slow and surprisingly even. Her lips were moving with silent words. She was just beautiful and I wondered if the moment of her death was imminent. As I stood in awe of this very spiritual scene I was suddenly startled by the sound of the doorbell and the sharp barking of Trudy's little dog. I longed to stay fixated on Trudy yet I had to answer the door to receive a small package from the postman. When I returned to Trudy's bedside with her dog cradled in my arms she opened her eyes with a soft gaze to me, smiled warmly and reached out her hand to hold mine. I shall always remember her words. They were full of excitement and delight, even through her weak voice. She said to me, "Oh Jean, I am so glad you came with me through the veil. Look, it's heaven! We are in heaven! Isn't this white light so amazing and look at all the magnificent colors! It must be God! Everything is so very beautiful here! And my little dog is with us too. Oh Jean, I am so happy! Heaven IS real!"

These were Trudy's own words that day. She continued looking around, gently turning her head from side to side, gesturing with her frail hands, with eyes softly gazing and face serene and ethereal. She invited me to help her look for her husband and son all the while commenting on how clear and radiant everything was.

I was astonished to hear that Trudy actually believed I had transitioned with her into this heavenly place she saw. I wasn't sure what to do or say to my transfixed patient. I prayed for the right words then gently told Trudy that I was standing next to her bed in the living room of her home with her dog in my arms. It was not her time to leave for her permanent home in heaven just yet and her dog and I needed to stay in this life for a while longer. She then opened her eyes fully and after a few moments of confusion she realized that she was indeed still here. She was quite disappointed. We talked about having faith and trust that her exact time to pass completely into heaven would come at just the right and best moment. With that comforting assurance Trudy fell into a deep sleep. When she awoke she told me that she vividly heard her husband's voice in a dream. He told her that he and their son would come for her on Thursday at 4 o'clock. She would be ready by then. It would be her right time to go.

Trudy stated this message with such assured conviction that I truly believed her. I felt very glad for Trudy because I knew that this was what she longed for and had waited for. I wanted to be there with her so I changed my schedule to make certain I was present to assist with her ease and comfort in making her final transition from this life to the next, the one which she had joyfully glimpsed several times. I left Trudy's home that day feeling excitement for her and sadness for me that the next time I saw Trudy would be the last.

The following night I was asleep when the ringing phone awakened me. As hospice nurses we all took turns being on call but this was not my week so I was not expecting a call at this time. It was Trudy's night nurse. She called to tell me that Trudy had drawn her final breath and easily and peacefully died at exactly 4 o'clock. I was stunned and a bit confused. My expectation was that Trudy would die at 4 p.m. on Thursday and that I would be there with her to say goodbye and witness the unfolding of her husband's prediction. It had never occurred to me that he meant 4 a.m.! Yes, it was Thursday and as I lay back in my bed I smiled, happy that Trudy's desire was fulfilled.

I lay there awake for a long time thinking about all that had happened and feeling very grateful to be a participant. Then suddenly I began to feel a distinctly warm energy surrounding me while at the same time becoming aware of a soft golden glow right in front of me. From this glow emerged an image of Trudy, smiling, nodding, and looking ethereal and serenely happy. I was so amazed and awed to actually see her and feel her presence. I knew for sure she was now with her beloved husband and son.....at last.

I did not sleep again that special night. I just lay there feeling gratitude for the awesome experience and blessing of Trudy in my life. As the sun rose in all its glorious splendor, splashing soft hues of red and gold into my bedroom, I realized how Trudy, my first hospice patient, had also been my partner in helping to strengthen my resolve to make a meaningful difference in the way a person can live out their final days and their moment of transition in peace and ease.

It was a manifestation of the meaning of the poem, "Teach Me to Die and I'll Teach You to Live". Trudy and I had done that for each other, and to this day I remain very thankful.

Diane's Story: A Light in the Storm

During my years as a hospice nurse I was intensely involved in caring for many terminally ill people in their own homes throughout all the phases of their dying process. My care included compassionately supporting patients and families with counseling, comfort measures, teaching aids, various in-home services and essentially, anything they needed. I knew it was right where I belonged. It had been my long time desire to make the final stage of life as comfortable and peaceful as possible for people.

People in the 1980's, and some even now in 2016, often thought of hospice as a desperate last minute recourse to attend to adults who were actively dying within hours or days. Doctors and families often waited too long to call for help because they didn't understand how hospice care could make that difficult time less stressful and more comfortable for patients and families over many months. Also, many people believed that to call hospice meant giving up or failing and being forced to accept death. Part of my job was to teach and encourage doctors, nurses, patients and families to take advantage of our many beneficial services as soon as possible after diagnosis of terminal disease. The hospice service within which I worked offered people much help and resources to live out their limited time as fully and as comfortably as possible. In those early days this type of nursing was not feasible in a sterile-like hospital setting with all its protocol and restrictions. Also, there were no separate respite facilities then. Home and its familiarities provided comfort and security to patients. Our hospice accepted all people including children who were given a year or less to live.

My previous pediatric experience made me the first nurse chosen to care for the children in hospice. I remember feeling anxious and doubtful about how well I could manage my own feelings in serving those most delicate patients and their families. Still lingering in my mind was the memory of the 12 year old girl who had suddenly, without warning, died in my arms many years earlier. I didn't have any chance then to prepare her or myself. So as a hospice nurse I prayed everyday for strength, courage and guidance in working with and assessing the immediate and ongoing needs of these special children in their anticipated dying process.

My most memorable of all young patients was Diane, a beautiful 9 year old girl who had, at my first visit, welcomed me with a maturity and poise of someone much older. There was a beautiful aura of gentleness and love around Diane that filled the room. This child knew that she had been given only a few months to live due to an inoperable brain tumor. Although she expressed sadness at soon having to leave her family she accepted her terminal diagnosis with bravery and grace.

From the first day I met Diane in summer of 1984, she and I began a relationship that grew closer and more special throughout the many months we spent together. I felt a most tender reverence in caring for her. We had many meaningful conversations during that special time. I was amazed at the depth of Diane's understanding of all aspects of life and its rhythms. She spoke knowingly of the nature of spirituality, of God's eternal love, and of her own soul's purpose which was to share that love. Diane intuitively knew the body, mind, spirit connection as well as the universal unity concept of oneness among all beings. Despite her young age and incapacitating illness, I often felt that she was my spiritual teacher with an intelligence, wisdom, grace, and sensitivity far beyond her years. I truly loved this exceptional child and I knew she loved me. It was such a blessing for me to be her nurse.

Throughout the months that Diane's physical condition increasingly deteriorated we both prepared for her death to be as gentle as possible. My heart was hurting along with Diane's and her family's. We decided to take each day as it came and make the most of it. Together we all made a plan to be present to each moment of everyday life, the joy and sorrow, laughter and pain. Diane believed as I did that there was something to be learned from each experience. Sometimes when her energy seemed to be a bit stronger, we played a game or used paints and crayons to draw and color. Diane enjoyed laughing especially at the antics of her little 4 year old brother who showered her with his affection. Diane's mother was very loving and attentive to her and always interested in how she could help me with Diane's care. She actually told me that she was thinking of becoming a nurse. I knew she would make a very good one.

In December about a week or so before Christmas, my sweet little patient was admitted to the hospital one last time with very little hope of her ever returning home. Diane's condition was grave. Before the ambulance arrived to transport her to the hospital she actually whispered to me that although she was not afraid to die, she would pray to outlive the doctor's prediction of her very brief timeline. Diane wanted to spend one more Christmas with her mother and little brother. She knew they were suffering too. It was a tremendous strain, especially at Christmas, for them to witness her dying process and to know that she would soon be gone from their lives. Also, her maternal grandmother was actively dying at this time and Diane felt that her own mother could not handle both deaths so close together. Nine year old Diane was praying for God to help her hold on. As desperately weak as she was, this brave and gentle child was still able to extend herself in an effort to help her mother and ease her family's distress. She was an inspiration to everyone who knew her.

I knew young Diane's spirit and faith were incredibly strong even as her body struggled to stay alive. I trusted that she would be able to hold on as she had prayed to do. So I was not too surprised to receive a call that she was going to be discharged from the hospital and, true to her own heart's wish, would be returned home by ambulance on Christmas Eve. I was thrilled to hear that news.

When the call came in I was sitting at my desk in the hospice office. Before I even had a chance to tell anyone near me, there was another call. This next one was a total surprise. It was from students at a local college who said they were going home for Christmas and wanted to give their decorated tree and ornaments to someone who could use them. Wow! I almost tripped getting out of my chair to share all the wonderful news with hospice staff. They knew about Diane being the only child we were serving at that time, so it was unanimous that these gifts would go to her. This was just perfect! I believed in the Divine Order of things and here it was in action! We were all excited. Factoring into this Divine Order was a friend who owned a business with trucks so I called him to explain the situation and ask for his help. He quickly arranged to have the tree and all decorations picked up at the college. I retrieved a key to Diane's home from her aunt so that we could keep this a surprise for my precious patient, her mom and little 4 year old brother.

My friend and I set up the tree with ornaments and lights, arranged all the decorations, and set out gifts I had bought for Diane and her family. I prepared her bed, put lighted candles in the windows, played Christmas music tapes on a "boom box" I had, and awaited her arrival home, set for 6 p.m. on Christmas Eve. My mind can still clearly see now, so many years later, Diane's face of joyous surprise as the EMT carried her up the stairs to her 2nd floor apartment. She looked all around in astonishment and wonder, smiling and uttering words of delight. With her mother and little brother following close behind, we all celebrated Diane's special surprise Christmas homecoming. For the rest of the evening I felt surges of love, joy, and deep gratitude for this gift of extended life and blessing for Diane and her family. The experience was priceless and, having brought along my Polaroid camera, I am thankful to have several cherished photos of that heart-filled evening.

After that special Christmas my nursing relationship with Diane continued with more frequent home visits to her, utilizing every available means to keep her comfortable. January was a quiet, reflective time. Diane's grandmother had died and Diane comforted her mother as well as she could as she continued to hold on to life. With trust and dignity she patiently waited for her own right time to transition to her spiritual home. I often thought that this sweet girl must have already visited there. She often spoke so confidently about spiritually profound truths with a deep love and wisdom that belied her age and fragile condition.

In late February 1985, as Diane's condition once more rapidly deteriorated, I suddenly became ill with a potentially cancerous tumor and was shocked to learn that I needed major surgery within days. I felt very upset that after all the time Diane and I had shared together I would be unable to be with her in her last hours. How could this be happening now? It was the worst possible timing for me. Other nurses assured me they would be with her and give her my final messages, yet I still felt distraught. Diane had been such an angel, an inspiration, a model of faith. If I now had to face cancer myself, would I be able to measure up to the strength, endurance, acceptance, and gentle love that this child had manifested throughout her illness? I felt sad, scared, inadequate, confused, and angry at the poor timing of it all. My personal faith in Divine Order was really being strained. My thoughts and feelings engulfed me and I prayed earnestly for strength, courage, acceptance, and understanding.

The day before my hospital admission I received a call that Diane had died quietly and peacefully in her home without me by her side where I had wanted and expected to be. I grieved about not being there, about the loss of my little angelic friend, and about the pain and loss her family was suffering. I wanted to at least see her family before my surgery so, going against my doctor's orders, I drove the short distance to her home and walked in.

There were many people, family and friends, consoling Diane's mother and each other. I noticed that in the corner of the room stood Diane's little 4 year old brother. He looked lost and alone, standing against the wall with slumped posture and downcast head and eyes. I went over to him, knelt down, and gently spoke his name. He looked at me with sad eyes and simply asked, "Does my sister still love me?" "Oh, yes," I assured him, "she loves you very much and she always will forever and ever." This sweet child breathed a heavy sigh of great relief and said, "Oh, thank you so much. I knew I could ask you, Ms. Jean." He smiled and hugged me tightly, then went outside to play.

It occurred to me then that I was meant to be right where and when I was most needed. Diane had not really needed me at the time of her death. Her little brother did. He knew that it was his sister's time to be with God. He knew that God loved everyone and that Diane loved God. Yet what was most important to him was to really know that his sister, now being with God, would still love him too.

The following day as I was being prepared for transfer to the hospital's surgical suite, something quite unexpected and wonderful happened. I was lying on the stretcher very much awake and alone in a dimly lit room, feeling apprehensive and waiting for the nurse to give me a sedative. Suddenly I was aware of a soft golden glow all around me. At first I thought someone had come in and turned on a light. Then to my amazement I literally saw Diane in her spirit form, translucent yet clearly defined, bright and shining. She was right in front of me. I saw her smiling at me and I absolutely heard her own voice whisper, " I'm here with you, Ms. Jean, don't worry, you will be just fine." I instantly relaxed and returned her smile, saying, "Thank you, sweetheart." I started to tell her I was sorry I couldn't be with her that last day but she had vanished.

As the medical team wheeled me into the operating room my face was still smiling and my heart was full of peace.

When I awoke in the recovery room I did not see Diane again yet I very clearly heard her say, " See, Ms. Jean, I told you, you really <u>are</u> fine and so am I. I love you, Ms. Jean." Just then the surgeon came in and said to me that he found no cancer and that I would be fine. I told him I already knew that because an angel had told me so.

Diane left me many spiritual gifts. I am honored, privileged, and humbled to have known and served such a beautiful soul. She also gave me a very special physical gift on that last Christmas Eve, a gift I treasure to this day. Her mother had told me that in early December Diane insisted her mom take her in her wheelchair to the few stores near her home to buy Ms. Jean a special gift. Her mother asked her what she was looking for and Diane told her that she would know it when she saw it. When Diane presented the gift to me that special Christmas Eve she said with her engaging smile that she chose a white candle lamp with a gentle stripe of pale blue and one of pale pink. We had once talked about the meanings of colors and I told her that blue represented peace, pink was love and comfort, and white was for Divine Light. Diane told me she felt that the candle she chose represented the light I had been to her in her storm. My heart was very deeply touched, for in truth this special angelic girl had been a light in my storm too.

I continue to feel deep gratitude for knowing Diane. Even now, so many years later, I feel my eyes mist as I look at the precious photos I have of her and of us together. In my closet is a laminated copy of the hospice story in which the local newspaper featured Diane, her family and me, published with photos in January 1985, the month before she died.

Farewell, dearest Diane. Your beautiful soul light shines forever in my mind and heart. It is my hope that sharing your story will be an inspiration to others. I am so glad to know we shall see each other again in that radiant Divine Light, far beyond any storm.

A Garden for Henry

While working as a hospice nurse in the homes of terminally ill patients and their families, I had many very memorable experiences. Although all of my patients remain special to me in my fond recalls, some of those patients found an extra special niche in my heart. One such person was Henry... a tall, slim and serious-minded man in his late 60's. He presented me with both challenge and privilege in my efforts to care for him, a care which began in the season of very early spring.

Before meeting Henry I learned some of his history from the physician who had assigned him to hospice care after making a diagnosis of terminal cancer. The physician was upset with himself because he had been treating Henry for what he believed to be a stubborn respiratory virus. When Henry failed to respond to several different therapies, further tests were ordered. The definitive diagnosis of end stage lung cancer was shocking to both doctor and patient. Henry's body was suddenly at war with a fast growing cancer that was exacting a huge toll on his body and making him endure debilitating weakness and pain. To make this ordeal worse for him was the fact that Henry always had a strict work ethic and spent all of his employable years working in a steel mill from which he had just retired before becoming ill. He had saved all his hard-earned money to fulfill a retirement dream of leisurely traveling cross country with his wife in a camper trailer they would purchase. Now his well planned dream trip was crumbling. The dual losses of his health and his dream were devastating disappointments to Henry, like bitter pills he fiercely resented having to swallow. He manifested this bitterness by sequestering himself in his bedroom, announcing that he would just wait to die in his bed. He refused all care and treatment by his doctor, by his wife, and by me. In fact during my first hospice visit I was angrily ordered by Henry to stay away from him. I agreed to do so at that time but told him I would return later to talk with him from the doorway. I then turned my attention to his wife Mary, who was given the same gruff order to stay away.

I vividly remember Mary. She was a small demure woman who was obviously quite upset and worried about her husband. Mary loved Henry very much. She knew the gravity of his condition and felt desperate to be with him, to care for him and comfort him. Understandably, she felt hurt, confused, and scared by his cold dismissal of her. I had often seen this reaction between spouses when their world was suddenly turned upside down. They simply did not know how to deal with their own overwhelming emotions and did not know how to relate to each other. It was up to me as hospice nurse to help them both.

In addition to caring for the patient another essential service of hospice nursing is caring for the needs of the patient's family members. This care includes skilled listening, therapeutic counseling, determining and implementing several necessary resources such as psycho-social support, spiritual or pastoral care support, nutritional planning, respite care from a trained volunteer, and home health aide services. In those early days of hospice there were no outside facilities that provided respite care for families nor were there any special care units in hospitals specifically designed for hospice patients. Today there are many such facilities in place.

On that initial visit, after Henry vehemently ordered his wife and me out of the room, the first thing I needed to do was to personally get to know my patient and his wife. Mary was emotionally upset and drained. She was basically alone with no family nearby and only a few neighbor friends who were unable to offer the kind of support she really needed. Mary and her husband had rarely been socially interactive with others throughout their long marriage, mostly due to Henry's disinterest and personally private nature.

Henry had his solid routine. He worked every day at the steel mill, he maintained the house and property, he planted and lovingly tended his annual vegetable garden, he read the newspapers, he watched favorite television shows at night with his wife, he tinkered with his tools in the basement, and he saved his money. Henry believed that as a husband he was solely responsible for earning all the money to provide for them and therefore did not condone Mary working outside their home. She accepted this and therefore spent her time cooking, baking, cleaning, and sewing. The few friends she did have were homemakers like herself. These women and their husbands were sympathetic to the news of Henry's terminal illness yet they were afraid and hesitant to become more than peripherally involved in supporting Mary and Henry's situation. Perhaps it reminded them of the fragility and vulnerability of their own lives. If this could happen to Henry, a hard working person like themselves, it could happen to them. Fear is powerful. It can often distance, restrict, numb, and immobilize people. In the 1980's most people feared even saying the word, cancer. Some people, even to this day, believe that cancer might be contagious. Some believe it automatically means a "death sentence" even though now there are many new diagnostic and treatment options that were previously unknown or unavailable.

In the early 1980's, the known regimens of chemotherapy and radiation were very harsh. Due to the aggressiveness and spread of Henry's lung cancer at the late time of his diagnosis, surgery was not an option. Henry refused any suggestion of other available therapies, namely, comfort and support measures that hospice could provide. His physician had insisted that Henry agree to a hospice nurse at least giving him medication for pain relief. He finally did so begrudgingly.

That first day I listened to Mary as she told me about the way she and Henry had lived their lives together and the various struggles they endured. They led a simplistic, orderly life and were committed to each other although they were not outwardly affectionate. While Mary felt sure that Henry loved her she knew that her husband was not really open to being romantic and admitted she missed having that comfort in their relationship. They had been married nearly 50 years, lived modestly in an old farmhouse surrounded by two acres of open land and had no children. Mary expressed that she still remained saddened by painful memories of several miscarriages in the early years of their marriage which led to the loss of hope for future viable pregnancies. She said after that time Henry became more somber in their relationship. She felt that her husband was deeply hurt by the losses and subsequent childlessness yet would never express his feelings. Unexpressed, buried grief becomes a hard and long held burden, which can block the ability to feel comfort and joy.

Mary told me that they also had to cope with some serious financial hardships along the way. Because of this Henry did not believe in taking vacations nor in spending money on "frilly non essentials" which he referred to as anything outside of the basics of daily living. They would wait until his retirement, which he deemed the "proper and deserved time" to take the big vacation and spend some money on pleasant indulgences. They had spent many hours discussing plans and details about this. Now with Henry's diagnosis and dire prognosis, their plans fell apart. Mary did not have any idea how to comfort her husband in his feeling of loss and grief, much less comfort herself. Henry's unexpressed grief from prior losses intensified the losses he now faced. Mary was especially afraid that his anger and resentment at "being cheated by life" would remain locked inside of him and keep him non-communicative and alienated from her until the day he died. She felt desperate to connect with him and was further stressed by not knowing how to do so.

Grief, fear and pain can change a person's outward expressions and behavior toward loved ones even as the internal depth of love remains strong. Although knowing this, Mary felt defeated by her husband's rejection and needed to gather her own sense of self to fortify her courage and strength. I taught her ways to physically and emotionally express her own painful feelings and fears. Some of those ways were through verbalizing and crying, through stress relieving exercises and stretches, through journaling and drawing, through calming and strengthening exercises, and through positive self-supportive affirmations and spiritual prayer. I offered Mary resources for helpful books and articles and gave her some useful ways to communicate with Henry. Those would help to calm him in his distress and allow him small measures of control. Having some personal control through simple everyday choices is very important to someone whose life is threatened by cancer or any terminal disease. This can help reduce feelings of fear, anger, and desperation. Reasonable choices can be made about food, bathing, body positioning, comfort measures, etc.

After conversing with Mary that first day we set a time for me to return the next day. Before leaving I checked on Henry. He was asleep, sleep which his wife said he desperately needed yet had been fighting. Perhaps he felt he could now sleep knowing someone was there for his wife. I stood in that doorway sending prayers, love, and healing energy to my patient. I knew that at least his spirit and soul would be accepting of these. I hoped and prayed that in time his mind and heart would follow.

The next day Henry again met me with resistance although he seemed just a bit less stubborn now at this second visit. After some gentle coaxing he did allow me to ask him, from the bedroom doorway, questions about his physical needs. He was moaning with much discomfort and I repeatedly assured him I could help. He began to cautiously accept that perhaps I could ease his pain. Eventually he allowed me into the room to administer medications and several comfort measures. I was grateful for this opportunity and for the ability to look into his eyes. I saw a very frightened, frozen man who was waiting to die. I knew I had to help Henry realize that he could learn to live out his remaining time on earth in ways that would make his dying process more comfortable and to perhaps even have some pleasant experiences. This would take time and trust and of course his willingness to have me and his wife care for him. Time was of the essence. According to the prognosis from his doctors and the cancer specialists, Henry's time line was very short. It was a frightening, sad and lonely situation for both Henry and Mary. In addition to utilizing all of my nursing skills and medical training, I prayed every day for spiritual guidance to lead my way in helping them both.

Throughout my life in the face of troubling events, sad and difficult situations, suffering, loss, grief, and death, I had questioned why. As my spirituality expanded so did my acceptance. I could let go of the daunting struggle to try to figure it all out by myself with the finite, limited understanding we humans have. This allowed me to believe that despite physical appearances to the contrary, the situations in one's life had to have some kind of positive meaning and purpose. God as the Universal Source had supreme understanding of it all. I had to trust in an All Knowing and All Compassionate Highest Consciousness God to know the entire scope and meaning of a person's life experiences. Often though, putting that faith into daily practice amid the deep suffering I so often witnessed was not easy. Yet without that faith and trust I would be lost. My prayer of healing for this couple and for everyone became affirmations for each person's highest good, most meaningful soul connection and spiritual growth, and as much body-mind comfort and peace as possible.

Working patiently with Henry day after day I was able to make small inroads to his trust in me. In the beginning the priority was pain relief and small, soothing comfort measures that allowed him to accept my return each day. I began attempts to have conversation with him about his life. Henry was resistant at first. Being a quiet, private man he was not accustomed to sharing his personal self with anyone, just as he was not accustomed to involving himself in other peoples' personal issues. He said that conversation didn't matter now because he was dying. I reminded him that as long as he was still living, his personal interests and personal philosophy of life continued to be very important and that I was especially interested in learning them. Although Henry seemed quite surprised by the last part of my statement he slowly began to respond. With proper medication combinations and nursing comfort measures Henry was able to feel less fearful and become more physically comfortable. Mary and I encouraged him to connect with his memories and relate them aloud at his own pace. With our support and some sustained convincing he finally agreed to try.

Henry's initial story surprised both Mary and myself. At first Henry's voice was weak and faltering and he needed rest periods in between several sentences. In his own time and way he showed us that he wanted to continue. Although my patient was weak and tired he began to express his long held grief about being childless, his shame and feeling like a failure to his wife. Compounding these feelings were the losses of his health and independence, his retirement plans with Mary, and his approaching death.

Over time Henry communicated more freely about all of these, although some days he was too weak. Still, he wanted to continue so after a day of rest he would re-open the dam that had held back his feelings. As Henry shared with Mary and me it was amazing to see how he became his own counselor. He said he finally understood the value of admitting and expressing his pain and forgiving himself. He felt that his willingness to do this was helpful to Mary too and indeed it was. Mary was able to feel a stronger connection with him and lovingly support all of her husband's brave efforts. There was no judgment.

Henry's courage and honesty allowed the opening of an inner space, a permission within himself, to then share his enjoyable memories. I was eager to continue listening to all his life stories, happy to know more about the man for whom I was caring. With each day Henry began to realize that his reminiscence and whispered storytelling gave him much needed release, a certain strength of mind, a higher degree of comfort, and some hope that he was still useful. A sense of purpose is indeed a vital part of a person's feeling of self worth and value.

When Henry talked about his great love of gardening I saw his face brighten and his whole being become more animated. Mary confirmed that this hobby had always been most relaxing, enjoyable, and empowering to Henry. When I voiced my interest in knowing details of his gardening experiences Henry seemed quite pleased, especially since it was the spring season at that time. From his bed confinement he shared every detail of how he used to stake out the garden area, prepare the soil, and plant the seeds of favorite vegetables. He would often express tearful sadness at being unable to do this again. The value of this emotional expression was that Henry's trust in himself and in me had reached his heart. He was revealing more of himself and in doing so, he was allowing healing, which literally means to make whole.... the integration of a person's body, mind, emotions, and spirit.

Healing is often mistaken by people to mean a cure. It's true that it sometimes does result in a cure. However, by its authentic definition healing is a process of re-integrating every aspect of a person's entire being of body, mind, emotions, and spirit back into the natural state of interconnected smooth, rhythmic and harmonious flow of energy and wholeness. This truth of healing may not include a physical cure yet it allows for the open full expression of living life and appreciating life to the maximum level of which one is capable. This fullness of living then enables the ultimate completion of physical life in a prepared, dignified, calm, peaceful dying process and death event. This process was one in which I felt so strongly called to serve as a hospice nurse and at the same time learn how to best apply these healing principles to my own life especially in my most wounded areas of personal brokenness.

Many weeks passed as Henry continued to release long held emotions and share his thoughts, ideas, memories, hopes, and feelings with both Mary and me. He became more relaxed and congenial, even laughing and joking at times. He was still gravely ill yet he was accepting his medical condition as terminal while allowing himself to live in each moment. This allowed him more freedom as well as strength and comfort. Henry began to easily cooperate and even offered to assist as he was able with treatments, medicines and nursing care. I gave him choices about these in whatever ways were safe and manageable for him. Henry had allowed the inclusion of a home health aide and a volunteer to give both himself and Mary some help and assistance. Eventually, he was able to tolerate being out of bed in a chair for short periods of time. Henry's relationship with his wife was expanding and growing with true intimacy as they learned healthy ways to converse and interact more honestly with each other in mutual love and respect. Mary became more relaxed and trusting. I was very happy to witness all of these beautiful healing manifestations.

One day in late spring Henry was sitting up in his wheelchair gazing out of the window as I made his bed and cleaned up after his bath. He was unusually quiet and seemed distracted. As I passed him at the window I could see his gaze following the outline of his well worn garden area. His entire countenance reflected sadness. Since he had been confined in the house for so long I suggested to Henry that we go outdoors where the weather was beautiful, sunny, and comfortably warm. The birds were chirping and singing the arrival of longer days. To my surprise Henry responded with enthusiasm. This was the first time he had even considered an outing and I was delighted for him. I wheeled him to the back porch and placed him at an angle where he could enjoy the sunshine yet be shaded. Then I realized that his bare garden plot was easily visible to him and that seeing it so clearly might cause him distress. I thought for a moment that to protect him I should turn him away. Then very suddenly as if by a strong intuitive guiding force I was compelled to leave him in that very spot. As Henry settled in his wheelchair and relaxed into the serene outdoor atmosphere he fixated on the garden spot. He began describing how he had first planted his garden so many years ago and how he had developed it each year to produce more hearty and delicious vegetables. Although Henry did all the tilling, preparing, and planting himself, he was quick to add that he and Mary often weeded and harvested the garden together, side by side. He also related how proud he was of her for expertly preparing and arranging his home grown vegetables for their meals. Clearly this garden was a unified effort of love and sharing, caring and nurturing, companionship and cooperation, accomplishment and pride. As Henry spoke that day I saw a resurgence of vitality, strength and hope that belied his grave physical condition. Mary noticed it too as she bustled about from kitchen to porch offering us refreshments. She was delighted that her husband was outdoors and more at ease. I shall forever remember when Henry suddenly turned to me with tears in his eyes and stated that he wanted to plant his garden, himself, one more time before he died. One more time would mean so much to him, he had said. He would have purpose.

Although I definitely believed in the importance of

Henry having purpose, my mind swirled with the impact of it all. What? Plant his garden? Himself? Now? How would he or could he do this? He wasn't able to walk or even stand steady on his feet and he tired so easily. I studied Henry's face as he kept his gaze focused on the area where he had always tended his garden. His eyes were intent, teary and dreamy. His breathing was a bit more rapid yet regular. He was smiling and I knew that in his mind he was creating his plan of how to do it. With a determined look and confident voice I heard this very ill and frail man tell me that he would begin the next morning. Just then Mary came onto the porch and had the look of shock on her face from what she had just heard her husband declare. Henry hadn't seen her so I signaled to Mary to go inside where we could talk and stand near the door to keep a watchful eye on Henry. Mary's hands covered her mouth in disbelief and emotion as I related her husband's entire conversation. He shared his fondest memories of their yearly garden ventures together, his pleasure and pride in that accomplishment and his deep yearning to have one more garden to relive those feelings. He needed to be useful and purposeful and proud again, doing what he loved one more time before his final day on earth.

The fulfillment of this soulful longing was a vital component in the process of true healing and wholeness even though I did not yet know how Henry's garden would begin to actually take shape. It was time for me to trust that Spirit would show us the way together. Mary joined in with her support and I marveled at the expansion of understanding, courage, and strength that she had demonstrated in the months I had known her. Mary cried her tears of many emotions, nodded her acceptance, went to Henry with her love and support to validate his desire, then helped me get him into bed to rest. Before I left their home that day I felt certain that Henry would have his garden. Upon my return the next morning we would begin crafting the plan. If the home health aide and the volunteer were willing, I would explain how much this garden meant to Henry and enlist their assistance in this very meaningful effort.

That next morning Henry was awake and smiling even though he needed his pain relief medicine. Of utmost importance of course was Henry's comfort for the day ahead. I immediately implemented the usual combinations of support. These included several medicines which allowed Henry to feel more comfortable and mentally alert, oxygen support, gentle bathing, and several physical positioning and comfort measures. Mary aided the effort by serving a small yet nourishing breakfast to her husband with kind and humorous encouragement for him to eat it all. Henry usually ate very little but that day, as a man set with his purposeful mission, he willingly complied. I suspected that he also intended to create this garden as a legacy for his wife....... another part of his healing journey.

With Henry settled in his wheelchair we went outdoors to the garden area. Mother Nature was very cooperative with her generous display of warm radiant sunshine, soft gentle breezes, and beautiful pale blue sky. The happy chorus of chirping birds added their lighthearted approval of our intention. Henry noticed it all with a smile and breathed a long sigh of contentment. He was ready. Considering that planting a small bed of string beans, tomatoes, peppers, and zucchini would be easiest, he began to sketch the plan on a drawing pad he held in his trembling hand. He relished the fact that these particular vegetables were his and Mary's favorites.

Even though I was so impressed by Henry's passion and determination I was very concerned about how the soil preparation and planting would actually be done. Because I had other patients to care for I was not able to increase my time at Henry's to undertake such a task alone. Mary agreed to do whatever prep work she was able to physically do and I could be of some assistance when I was there but we'd need more help. When the home health aide and the volunteer were made aware of this plan they both replied with an encouraging "Yes, let's do this for Henry!" Meanwhile, Mary had spoken with her neighbor friends about her husband's deep desire to have this garden and they, along with their husbands, offered to help. We had a team! Henry would be the creator, the foreman, the leader of his final victory garden. The plan was all coming together in a beautiful way. With everything in place the work began. Henry was in high spirits. He was surrounded by his loving wife, his supportive neighbors and friends, and his dedicated caregivers. Henry's heart was open to receiving this outpouring of love and he welcomed it. The transition from angry, scared, and frozen man who wanted only to die alone to a man whose entire being was now shining with love, acceptance, and joyful purpose was truly remarkable.

During my hospice nursing experience I had often witnessed the phenomenon of terminally ill patients gaining a certain strength and far outliving the time line projected by doctors. In every case there had been a personal goal that the patient was determined to see come to fruition. These goals ranged from being present at a child's wedding to finishing a college degree to reuniting and reconciling with an estranged family member. Every single story of these accomplishments filled me with joy and deepened my respect for the indomitable strength of the human spirit and soul. Henry's special story had some unique and amazing qualities.

I communicated to Henry's physicians his garden plan and accompanying excitement and determination. Of course they were extremely skeptical of Henry's ability to follow through and they strongly disapproved of such an outrageous idea, even forbidding it! They reminded me of the gravity of his condition and the very short terminal status they predicted. I told them that despite these outward signs of impending death, Henry's spirit was leading the way for him to realize his dream. I added that those of us helping him as a team supported him in this fulfillment. The positive energy surrounding Henry strengthened his own energy. His focus on this beloved project was in itself a pain reliever and relaxant for him. His physicians finally relented and became reluctantly accepting of Henry's endeavors to realize his fervent last wish. I promised to keep them aware of his progress and outcome.

Everyone on the team participated in fun and cooperative ways until the planting was finished and Henry was satisfied and grateful. Henry's next desire was to see the fruits of everyone's labor culminate in a grand vegetable harvesting, the activity of which he intended to lead himself. I must say that I did wonder along with everyone else if Henry's life could possibly extend to that time which was still a few months away.

We all continued to care for Henry in various ways with our individual helping roles. Henry became more frail and debilitated as the disease continued to ravage his body. There were many days when Henry was too weak to be in the wheelchair. At those times Mary and I pushed his bed to the window and elevated his head so that he could see his garden growing, This small act brought him contentment and a measure of renewed strength if only for a few moments.

When I had originally offered to channel to Henry the comfort and pain relief modality of healing energy he had refused because he did not accept the concepts of holistic healing. However, after seeing his garden planted he revisited the idea and decided the concepts had much personal merit as evidenced by his own experience. My patient then invited me to channel to him in the hopes that it might strengthen him enough to see his garden be harvested. I was delighted to comply. Henry received this healing method of Reiki each day and commented on how it comforted and strengthened him beyond what he could have imagined.

Soon the anticipated time came when the first vegetables were ready. It was a very exciting day when Henry felt strong enough to be in his wheelchair to be pushed outdoors to the garden's edge. I shall forever remember the moment when Henry reached out to pick the first tomatoes and green beans and held them in his hands like precious jewels. His tearful smiles of joy, pride and gratitude were priceless. Against all odds Henry had accomplished his final goal. He had not been able to take his wife on the retirement vacation he had planned yet he was able to give his beloved Mary a far more meaningful gift.....the wonderful yield of their special garden, grown and nurtured together with love and tenderness. Witnessing and participating in the unfolding of Henry's healing process from the first day I met him until this day of fulfillment was indeed a miracle to remember and cherish.

Henry's last meal was a few spoonfuls of delicious soothing broth of his garden vegetables made with the loving, dedicated hands and heart of his grateful wife, Mary. The following day Henry died gently and peacefully in Mary's arms. As I witnessed Henry's death I felt humbly proud and privileged to be by the side of this beautiful couple as they completed the final phase of their most powerful and loving journey together. Henry's last words to his wife were, "Don't worry, we'll be together again, Mary. I'll be waiting for you on the other side."

"LOOKING FOR SPACE"
Words and Music by John Denver

.....Words of the Song's Refrain.....

"AND I'M LOOKING FOR SPACE
AND TO FIND OUT WHO I AM
AND I'M LOOKING TO KNOW AND UNDERSTAND.
IT'S A SWEET, SWEET DREAM,
SOMETIMES I'M ALMOST THERE
SOMETIMES I FLY LIKE AN EAGLE,
AND SOMETIMES I'M DEEP IN DESPAIR."

Gifts from a Night Time Visitation

One time during the early years of my soulful journey, as I finished my busy hospice nursing workday, I was confronted with a startling reality. A number of unforeseen circumstances very suddenly and unexpectedly left me without a place to live! It was a shocking, numbing feeling. What should I do? Where should I go? Why was this happening? I had to forcibly rouse myself out of the limbo to act quickly. Night was approaching. So there I was in the darkening dusk of evening packing everything I could into my car, feeling alone and confused by the suddenness of it all. It was too late and my circumstance too strange to call a friend so I spent that first night in a small motel feeling upset and unable to sleep. I knew I had to find more stable residence immediately but efforts to find a place to live would need to wait until after my work the next day. I prayed for guidance and protection, courage and confidence in locating the next right place for me. I also prayed for calmness to quell my shakiness. I needed to keep breathing deeply and consciously choose to replace each wave of anxiety and distress with trust and belief that I would be safely directed by Spirit. I also prayed to believe that this scary experience somehow had a larger purpose and meaning for me. Despite all my praying, positive affirmations, and efforts to relax, sleep seemed impossible that night. Morning was quickly approaching and I knew that at 8 a.m., after first stopping at the hospice office, I had to be alert, calm, focused and ready to travel out to the homes of my patients to take care of them. Guardian angels and the extra charge of my body's adrenalin would have to keep me going.

As I entered my office early the next day I had a feeling that perhaps my coworkers would be able to offer some ideas. I loved my job and the people with whom I worked. I knew they'd help if they could. The hospice office was staffed with a kind and caring secretary who, being there early like me, was browsing through the local newspaper before the start of our workday. As she greeted me she commented that I looked tired and stressed so I told her my story of needing to find an immediate place to live. She was very empathetic and comforting, even offering me to stay in her home for as long as I needed. I was grateful for her support yet I felt compelled to search for a place right away. Then my friend remembered that she had just seen a rental ad in her newspaper for a furnished room. It was in a safe neighborhood home, offering use of all amenities of the house for a reasonable rate with a month to month lease. She excitedly said the ad had just caught her eye and she didn't even know at that moment why she had paid attention to it. Wow! I knew why.....Divine assistance to my rescue!

I called the number and spoke with the home owner whose voice sounded kind, friendly and sincere. I would meet him to see the house right after work that day. As soon as I arrived I knew it was the place for me to be, temporarily. For the long term I would rent an apartment, so living here for a while would give me time to search .for the best one. I moved in that day. The house had all the things I needed and even included a swimming pool which I enjoyed for the remaining few weeks of summer. My bedroom and bathroom were upstairs and the room across the hall was being rented by a college student. He was far from home and very happy to have an older person with whom he could relate as a stand-in parent or mentor. This worked out fine. I felt welcomed and safe in the house and it was close to my hospice office.

As summer faded into autumn there was an early and persistent damp chill in the air that seemed to seep right into my bones. For as long as I can remember my body never did acclimate very well to dampness and cold. Each day as the damp chill continued with lowering outdoor temperatures down to 44 degrees at night I felt really cold, making it very difficult to sleep. Also, I was alone in the house. My college housemate was staying at school for his first few weeks and the owner of the house was away on a long business trip. He had set the thermostats in the house to begin heat in the third week of October. This was only the first week in October and each thermostat was covered with a locked plate so it was impossible to turn on any heat before the set date. The home owner was on the road, traveling from place to place for his job. There were no cell phones in the mid 1980's so I was unable to talk with him until he called to check on the house. He did call in that first week but to my dismay did not offer a remedy for my situation other than more blankets. The key to unlock the plates on the thermostats was with him. He declined to send it, saying he'd be home before that 3rd week in October. Of course that was no help to me at the time! For safety reasons he did not allow any space heaters in the house. Being an outdoorsman himself I really believe he just didn't understand how I could feel so cold. Even the use of several extra blankets was not a solution for me. Hot tea, hot chocolate and even plain hot water gave me only short respites. I remained quite uncomfortable. It actually felt warmer outside of the house than inside.

My hospice nursing job was intense and often emotionally exhausting. I needed to be well rested to take good care of my patients and their families. Yet lack of sleep due to being so cold at night made me feel more tired and stressed. I tried to meditate and visualize warmth into my body, all with little success. I was frustrated and disheartened. Here was another challenge that I didn't understand. I had been so sure that this was the perfect place for me to stay, that Spirit had guided me here, so why did I have to deal with this additional uncomfortable situation? What was this supposed to teach me? I felt justified in yelling out loud to God that this was unfair and undeserved and I let myself wallow in that for a bit. It's just what I'd tell my patients to do as a healthy method of release. An outburst was a good and important emotional release which then allowed me the space to reassess my complaining. I realized that this situation of mine was temporary. There were so many people and places in the world with much more serious problems and those who had no hope of any warmth at all. I stopped complaining and returned to my spiritual resources.

Once again I replaced each wave of distress with trust that I would be led by Spirit and be shown a larger purpose and meaning that would help me grow in self and soul awareness. I hate being cold so dedication to believing all this was a really big stretch for me this time. Still, even while huddled under blankets and often shivering, I persisted in my positive affirmations as I prayed for acceptance of the situation and some good ideas to get warm!

One late night when I was unable to fall asleep, feeling particularly weary, lonely and cold, a strange sensation began to embrace me. It was a strong yet gentle warmth penetrating the cold in my body. At first I thought that the thermostat must have somehow turned on the heat. But there was absolute quiet in the house, with no sound of a heater coming on. I got up to check the thermostat. It was turned off with the hard cover still intact. No heat had come on so where was this warmth coming from? I could now feel it all over the room. Becoming a little nervous I walked around looking for some kind of heat source when suddenly the light bulb in my bedside lamp blew out. No other lamp was working either. This made me really nervous so I quickly climbed back into bed and pulled the blankets tightly around me as a sort of protection from the unknown. I lay there in the black darkness continuing to feel distinct warmth, taking long slow breaths to calm myself and praying for safety as well as a plausible answer to this mystery.

Within minutes there appeared a glowing ray of pale green light cascading into the room from above my bed near the ceiling. I watched in awe as this light flowed down and filled the space at the foot of my bed. All anxiety immediately left me and was replaced by a feeling of calm amazement as I saw the shimmering green light instantly take form as ten distinct images. Each one was shaped as a beautiful, tall angelic-like being, each of whom radiated out to me sparkling beams of a deepening jade green light. These beings surrounded my bed and enfolded me in an energy of warmth and love and peace that is even now, nearly indescribable. I was aware I could not move any part of my body. I tried in vain several times to move some part of myself. I could not move at all. I felt totally paralyzed yet very safe, awake and alert to the entire incredible experience. I cannot say how long this lasted. Time had stopped for me and I was unaware of anything else. There were no words spoken, yet the ten angelic light beings were offering me penetrating warmth, total relaxation, comfort, and a deep sense of well being. They continued their blessed gift to me until I began to feel sleepy. Then slowly the beings became indistinct as they blended together and floated up to the ceiling in the same way they had arrived, as a glowing ray of pale green light. They then faded and disappeared. I lay there remembering that the color green has the spiritual meaning of healing, hope, and new beginnings. I had prayed for these to manifest in my life along with a way to feel warm, yet never expected to actually see angels sent to give me these gifts! This was a God demonstration beyond my imagination. I was truly awestruck at this experience.

My intention right afterward was to mentally replay every detail of what had happened before falling asleep and to write it down. Yet it was all so very relaxing and comforting that I quickly and easily drifted into a very sound sleep and awakened in the morning feeling refreshed, happy, healthy, confident, and comfortably warm. I clearly remembered everything and never again experienced being cold in that house, despite another 10 days of no heat and persistently damp weather with cold temperatures.

Upon awakening in the morning after that mystical experience I intuitively knew that my next place to live would soon be made known to me and catapult me into adventures and discoveries that would further expand my growth. I did not know exactly what these would be, yet I felt excited. In following years the gifts from that amazing angelic visitation would continue to multiply in my life with their appearances at opportune times and in surprising ways.

Sure enough, two months later the next major change occurred. However, I had hoped this one would not happen. My hospice workplace was forced to close due to persistent underfunding. This resulted in its inability to continue carrying the financial burden of all the people we served, some of them at minimal or even no cost. At that time there were no other hospices operating anywhere in or near my area so I had to return to hospital nursing. My intention was to utilize my skills there even though it was an environment unfamiliar with the specialties of hospice nursing. My thinking was that perhaps I could be a leader there for implementing the philosophy of holistic hospice care to patients regarded as terminally ill. Although the private hospice was a sad loss for me, I felt certain I would be spiritually led through the transition as long as I had a willingness to trust the process.

In the hospital setting there were staff members who challenged me for trying to introduce a practice that was more comprehensive and time consuming than the routine patient care to which they were accustomed. Thankfully, some progressively minded nurses were immediately interested. They started asking me to give them information and examples of how to more effectively, more confidently, and more comfortably give their patients compassionate end-of-life care. I was delighted to set up small informal groups of instruction for them after our shift. It was a slow process yet it was a good start. I had always enjoyed teaching and sharing what I knew to be helpful. My disappointment was that hospital administration was not at all supportive of my efforts at that time.

Soon there was another new beginning for me. It was

time to leave the house I had lived in for the prior 6 months and move into a more substantial place of my own. One day before Christmas while randomly browsing through a newspaper, a particular ad immediately grabbed my attention. It offered an apartment with a $100 discount on rental for the first 3 months and included everything I needed, even a balcony overlooking a serene meadow. It seemed perfect. I moved into the apartment in early January. That lovely place became a wonderful haven for me to learn more about myself, my spiritual nature, and my evolving soul purpose. However, the way this began was unexpected. Three months after I was in my new home I seriously injured my back while lifting a paralyzed patient in the hospital. That compounded the strained and weakened spinal areas from previous back injuries which made me definitely unable to return to hospital nursing. Here I was again, needing to figure out what this new injury meant!

The body has a unique way of communicating messages from the soul. It was telling/showing me that I needed to move into another phase of my career. On some level of consciousness I knew that. I had been struggling with an idea of leaving the hospital to pursue teaching classes about holistic health, incorporating everything I knew to help people in a more personal and complete way. My intention was to include metaphysical concepts, hospice care, energy healing, meditation, and body, mind, spirit integration counseling. This is what I really wanted to do yet I vacillated with a decision. Was I really up to the challenge? Would enough people be interested? Did I have sufficient skill to do this alone? Could I sustain an adequate income? Once again in my life, my body stopped me in place so I would really understand the message to make the decision for change. Oftentimes physical body drama is what it takes to go with the choice you intuitively know is the right one to make yet feelings of fear, guilt, insecurity or old familiarity keep you on the fence.

So there I was, alone and physically incapacitated for a while, having to be still and listen for spiritual guidance. That reflective time and my cozy apartment provided me with the space to be inspired. Spirit guided me to my next phase of growth, which enriched my spiritual, holistic, and metaphysical studies and prepared me for sharing these with others. I was on my way to a new place again with more gifts from the visitation.

All kinds of ideas came into my mind and I felt the excitement of a new creative energy. My first venture was the design of an eight week course in meditation and relaxation. During this creative spurt my back injury was healing, so my handwritten work was done going from positions on recliner to bed to sofa, to floor. When it was finally completed I presented my course to a local college. At first the college was quite hesitant to allow such "unusual and questionable" classes but after interviewing me and inspecting my handwritten syllabus, they agreed to give me a trial run. To their surprise and mine the classes were filled with waiting lists of students eager to receive this information. Also to my surprise and delight, several students in my first class asked me for private tutoring of holistic concepts and healing energy sessions. I felt sure this was my path now and I was happy to step onto it. Word quickly spread and very soon I was in the beginning of what became a long time successful private practice of offering individualized holistic healing and counseling to clients. This felt so right for me.

However, in those early days there was a challenge I had not thought about. Since I had no business plan and no experience in the financial, bookkeeping or legal aspects of being self employed, I needed help. My prayers started with a thankful attitude and belief that just the right person would soon be appearing for me. Spirit was there with immediate assistance. The following day I saw an ad in the "Job Wanted" section of the newspaper for a part time bookkeeper. Phyllis was just perfect. She was a very lovely older woman and well experienced in her field. She very quickly assessed my need for more help and organization than I ever expected! Phyllis was very kind and understanding of my situation. She even generously volunteered her services to get me started. She was wise, non-judgmental and supportive to me in many ways. Over the many years working together as professionals, Phyllis and I developed a strong bond of personal friendship, respect, trust and support. It has been my honor and joy to know this great woman and to share stories of our lives and families. Phyllis is now 95 years of age, healthy and strong. We continue to enjoy this cherished relationship for which I feel very blessed and deeply grateful. One aspect of faith is trusting that the right people come into your life at the right time. Some are there for a single reason. Some are there for a certain season. Some are there for a lifetime, which is where Phyllis belongs in mine.

More gifts continued to manifest. During the same time period as my private practice was evolving, I developed many other holistic classes, workshops and courses. It was rewarding to have taught them all for many years at the college as well as at various other institutions and facilities. One of my favorite experiences was creating experiential classes for groups in a program called, "Tuesday College for Women". Additionally, I studied and implemented several new healing modalities with clients and students. I hosted and led weekly meditation groups, formed metaphysical and healing discussion groups with new friends, and became a Certified Imago Relationship Therapist for couples, singles, and families. It was so rewarding to guide people through quality, highly effective communication skills in a format designed by Dr. Harville Hendrix Ph.D. The outcomes in peoples' lives with this therapy were positively successful. In my heart I felt proud of how my professional and personal skills had expanded my understanding of so many aspects of life and relationships. I wished I had known this many years earlier. Yet, to regret not knowing something before one is able or ready to know, is futile and a waste of vital energy.

I shall always feel very grateful for that especially tender night time visitation, for all the blessings and gifts given to me then and thereafter, and for the eternal presence, guidance and unconditional love of God, my angles and spirit guides throughout every moment of my existence. That glorious angelic visitation has remained vibrant and secure in my heart and soul memory for all these years. I share it here for the very first time with extra special gratitude.

When we are open to trusting that what we ask for in faith shall be given, we can then allow the receiving of it in God's Divine order, timing and way. We can see, feel, experience, and know for a fact that our request is answered in the best possible way for our highest good. Spirit is always present, ready, willing and able to attend to the details of our needs and desires. It is our responsibility to hold the vision of receiving the end result and trusting that it is on its way in just the right time, place, and manner. If there are unexpected detours and challenges, they can be opportunities to learn important lessons along the path to the desired outcome. Life is a sacred journey, a remembrance of the Truth of who we are in our continuous co-creative partnership with Divine Source. I had been taught that seeing is believing. Then I experienced that believing is seeing. There are very many examples of this in my everyday life now. They no longer surprise me for they have become the norm for me. I recognize each serendipity as a flow of grace and alignment with Source in that moment. It makes me smile every single time and delight in giving immediate thankful appreciation as I say to the Universe, "Yes, I'll have more of this please!"

My Personal Visit with Louise Hay

This book of mine may never have been written for publication if it were not for a very special time when I was privileged to share a personal visit with my cherished mentor, Louise Hay.

I had read her first book, "You Can Heal Your Life" as soon as it was published in 1984. I was very excited to realize that she had a holistic philosophy like my own. Louise had utilized that philosophy to heal herself of cancer through understanding the disease's corresponding mind, body, emotion and spirit components and what she needed to do to bring balance to her whole self. I immediately felt a strong connection to Louise and repeatedly read her writings, and listened to her cassette tapes and conference presentations.

In a short time Louise became well known in the metaphysical and spiritual circles in which I was involved. I once attended a lecture she gave in Philadelphia, PA and wanted to run right up to her to tell her of my admiration for her and the soul connection I felt with her. Of course I wasn't able to go backstage at that time so I convinced myself then that someday I would really meet her in person.

During the time I read Louise's first book, I was a hospice nurse and was seeking ways to more fully assist my patients with their struggles in preparing to die. I knew it was important for me to understand what each patient's own spiritual belief was and how they did or did not rely on it to help themselves. I also sought to more deeply understand their thought patterns and belief systems as well as their longings and fears. The experiences and wisdom shared so beautifully by Louise helped me to more personally individualize the care of my patients. Additionally, the loving guidance, support, and encouragement of this wonderful teacher, healer and great lady provided me with skills to better manage my own personal life challenges.

In 1988 I became extremely ill and had a profound near death experience, all of which I have recounted in a chapter of this book. One day during my long recovery I found a forgotten receipt for discounted air travel to anywhere in the USA. It had been in a drawer since before I became ill. The travel deal was a promotion by a local food store that entitled the purchaser of a certain dollar amount of food in a certain time frame to gain roundtrip airfare for $89. When I found the ticket I was still quite weak from the illness but I was determined to redeem this opportunity to go to California. The receipt was about to expire so I had to make plans quickly.

One of the first things I knew I wanted to do was

to contact Louise Hay. It was early 1989. Hay House publishing company's address and phone number were in the front of Louise's book. I called the number to say I would be writing Louise a letter to ask for a private meeting with her when I was in California. I remember the phone receptionist sounding surprised that I was so sure that this would actually happen. Then I followed through with the letter and called back to make sure Louise received it and read it. Being such a gracious lady, Louise herself returned my call and invited me to meet privately with her. We planned for 20 minutes before the start of her weekly Hay Ride gathering, which was devoted to helping people who were suffering with AIDS. Some of their families and friends would be there too. At that time, AIDS was an often fatal, misunderstood disease that created fear, bias and harsh judgment in people around the world. Louise was a genuine pioneer in supporting tolerance, understanding, comfort and healing to those who suffered.

Although still feeling physically weak, I was very excited as I traveled alone to California for the first time. My body felt supported by my strong resolve to make this special journey. I arrived in enough time to rest and prepare to meet my beloved luminary. True to her word Louise was there at our pre-set meeting time. It was a lovely day in West Hollywood so we sat outdoors in an alcove at a small table together. I told her of my sincere admiration and deep gratitude for her work. I told her of my own personal and professional work with the same holistic philosophy. I told her of my recent serious illness and its impact on my life and my frustration with the slow recovery. She invited me to share this with the participants in the Hay Ride gathering that evening. I was hesitant to accept. My situation was different from theirs. Although weakened by my illness I had almost fully recovered while most of them had been told they would not recover. What could I possibly say to them that would be helpful? Louise encouraged me to join the group, tell my story, and receive the healing love that she said always flowed there. She was certain that I could also be of some help to others. I trusted her.

As I walked into the building I was amazed to see nearly 300 people gathered in a large open space that I seem to remember as the gym in a high school. The people were being given song sheets and candles to hold as they sat in concentric circles with Louise in the center. Around the perimeter of the large room were tables of books and cassette tapes of songs and affirmations by Louise and others who had recorded with her. Everyone was kind and friendly so I introduced myself as a visiting kindred spirit from the east coast.

At the start of the Hay Ride we all became quiet and held our candles as we were led into a most beautiful meditation by Louise, which was made extra special with her soothing voice and calming presence. Then I remember singing together as a group yet I don't remember whether we sang after the meditation or before the close of the evening. One of the songs entitled "I Love Myself The Way I Am," was exceptionally powerful for me. It touched my heart and I became tearful, feeling compassion for everyone there, including myself. The person next to me whom I had never before met, put his arm around my shoulder in an expression of support and kinship.

The rest of the evening was filled with people relating their personal stories of illness, isolation, fear, shame, despair. Yet with each story there were immediate responses from others of acceptance, support, understanding, hope, and inspiration. So with Louise's encouragement I gathered my own courage and shared my story of the effect that my serious illness had on me with feelings of shame and guilt, frustration and depression. Even though I did not have HIV or AIDS, everyone there who did suffer with those illnesses treated me with the same respect, kindness and compassion. We all felt common emotions and feelings. Being part of the Hay Ride community that evening was truly an amazing and heartwarming experience of witnessing and experiencing authentic human and spiritual love. It was an incredibly wonderful, caring and beneficial evening that I shall always remember.

A few years later I taught the "I Love Myself" song to my then 5 year old nephew Ryan. He loved to sing and was very eager to learn this particular song. After Ryan memorized the entire multi-versed song in three days, he and I sang it together for the family while his dad, my youngest brother Buddy, recorded it. That memory, captured so well in the video tape, is precious to me. Over the course of many years I shared with my clients and students Louise's special love song as well as her fun song,

"On the Road to Prosperity " and her other tapes, CD's, books, affirmation calendars, and website offerings. So many of those people voiced to me their appreciation for being given the opportunity to learn from her.

That day in spring of 1989 as Louise and I ended our very special time together she told me that she believed the story of my spiritual journey was important to tell and that if I wrote it down in a book someday, her own company, Hay House, would publish it. So here I am, 27 years later, finally writing my book and feeling honored to have Balboa Press, the self publishing division of Hay House, helping me to share my stories with the world.

Louise Hay truly helped me to grow, mature, and feel supported as I traveled the often lonely path to finding my authentic self through embracing and living the deep and persistent call of my soul. To this day I continue to find Louise's philosophy, her wisdom, her voice, her affirmations, her songs and her insights remarkably inspiring and comforting. With all my heart I thank you Louise, for meeting with me and for sharing your beautiful self, your grace, your encouragement and your wisdom for so many years. I shall always admire you and remain one of your greatest and most grateful fans.

Almost to the Light:
My Near Death Experience

In August, 1988 I was totally unprepared to learn that I was as ill as I really was. For several weeks I had not felt well but dismissed the vague multiple symptoms with the assurance to myself that I was just tired from working too much. I had my own full time private practice as a holistic health counselor, therapist, and educator, was also creating and teaching classes at local community colleges and organizations, and leading two weekly meditation groups in my home. I was very busy doing all that I believed I had been spiritually called to do.

Personally, I was grieving the recent death of my sister's infant baby who very sadly died that last day of April after months of suffering from a harsh terminal illness. My heart ached for my sister and her husband. I felt so inadequate in my efforts to help my baby nephew during his illness and to comfort my beloved sister and brother-in-law. Two weeks earlier our maternal grandmother, to whom I was very close, had also died. My mother needed comfort and support as she coped with the loss of her own mother as well as her grandson, whom she helped deliver into the world. It was a very difficult time for all the family.

In July I had started to lose weight. At first it didn't concern me. I had been taking a combination of herbs, most of them for cleansing, in an effort to be a more clear channel for all the energy work I was doing with others every day. Then my appetite for food diminished. Being a nurse I knew that I needed to make time to eat whether or not I was hungry or had any appetite. Still, having such a busy schedule, I ate sporadically and did not pay much attention to those early clues of impending illness. Gradually more symptoms surfaced as mild abdominal discomfort and intermittent nausea. My thought was that perhaps I had a gall bladder problem. After all, that did run in my family. Oh well, I'd make time to go to the doctor next week or the week after that. I had so much going on in my life, in my family, and in my holistic work that I told myself this was no time to be sick and that I'd just do some healing on myself.....when I got the chance.

As July passed into August I felt extremely tired everyday and had an aching back as well as an increase in abdominal discomfort. So in between my client sessions I would lie down and immediately fall asleep, only to be awakened by the doorbell announcing my next client. Of course I pretended to be fine even as I prayed for help to get through each day. I had been teaching classes to women on good practices of self care and nurturing, an idea in which I truly believed. I assured them that regularly practicing those good habits would result in better health and well being for themselves. They deserved to feel their best and to be happy. Yet here I was, trying my best to nurture others, teach them how to nurture themselves and, in the meantime, had neglected my own self care. Finally, I could no longer avoid the truth when one of my clients, who had been out of town for a month, came for her appointment with me. I opened the door to hear her startled gasp as she exclaimed how extremely thin and pale I looked and that the white sclera of my eyes was yellow! I ran to a mirror and was shocked to really see myself as she saw me. How had I not even noticed? Now I was scared. My delay in getting a medical exam sooner was a huge mistake. However, still being in some denial, I reassured myself that all I'd need was treatment for a sick gallbladder and I'd be okay.

My client and I agreed to reschedule her appointment. Little did I know then that I would be unable to return to my work for a year. That same day I called a friend who was also a physician. We had not seen each other for some time and it so happened that a week earlier she and I had planned a visit for that evening. I asked her to come a little early. Upon seeing how I looked she gave me a quick exam and told me that since my liver felt enlarged and inflamed I possibly had hepatitis, rather than gall bladder disease. I really did not want to believe this. She ordered tests to be done the following morning, massaged my aching back and sent me to bed. She needed to leave for an out of state conference later that night and said her colleague would follow up with me.

When I awoke in the morning I was so ill that I literally could not get out of bed. I called my sister, also an RN, at her workplace. Hearing my distress she called my parents who drove the distance to my apartment. They both gasped as soon as they saw me. I must have looked wretched to them. My parents insisted on taking me to their doctor in the town in which I grew up. He was known as an excellent diagnostician. When we arrived at his office I had prompt blood tests there which confirmed a severe case of hepatitis, an inflammatory infection of the liver. My doctor immediately admitted me to the hospital where I remained a patient for 16 long uncomfortable days. The hepatitis was diagnosed as type Non A-Non B, which the doctor later discovered was caused by a cytomegalovirus. His medical team decided that the virus' severe impact on my liver probably had its origin in a delayed reaction to post surgery blood transfusions I received 3 years earlier. I had reacted very badly to the second unit of blood at that time due to an incompatibility with the donor's blood proteins. Cytomegalovirus is a rather common and benign virus in most people's own blood, so it can be in a donor's blood and be transferred unknowingly into the person receiving the transfusion. The virus can lay dormant, causing no symptoms, until that person's immune system becomes so weakened from the body being too stressed and exhausted to deal with it. Then the inflammatory potency of the virus dramatically worsens. That was my situation. Also, the doctor said the herbal combination I had been taking at home most likely contributed to my illness. I didn't believe the herbs could be a problem until later when I found out that I was allergic to some of them so the herbal allergy further weakened my immune system.

During my hospital stay I had much pain and nausea and felt extremely weak. My skin and eyes were golden yellow. There was bruising all over my body due to the lack of Vitamin K whose production in the liver was interrupted by the infection. Treatments included continuous bed rest, 60 bottles of IV fluids, and several medicines to combat the inflammation. My doctor was very concerned about how sick I was and told my family that any recovery would be long and slow. I was miserable. I worried about just how long my recovery would take, when I would be able to return to work, and how I would support myself in the meantime. I also worried about my clients. I felt terrible for suddenly leaving them without warning and no idea when I could return to my private practice to continue helping them. I also felt so guilty that I had pretty much ignored my symptoms for too long and now everyone was paying a price. My distress escalated knowing my children had to see me in that state. I was depressed. Everything was such a mess.

My family visited with their loving support, made jokes to get me to smile, and encouraged me to eat anything at all to gain some strength. I had zero interest in food of any kind. I tried my best to join in lighthearted conversation with family and friends but I was too sick and weak to last very long in this effort. Several friends traveled the distance to see me, pray with me, sing to me, and cheer me up. Friends offered to take care of things for me in my apartment and relay the message of my grave illness as the reason for my sudden absence. They made a phone chain to elicit prayer support. Although I was truly grateful for all this caring and support, my overwhelming feeling was despair. I blamed myself. I felt guilty, ashamed, vulnerable, and very sorry for betraying my own beliefs in the importance of self care. I was angry at myself yet refused to feel like a victim or a martyr. I would not give up. All I could do now was surrender to my situation, pray for guidance and to be willing to listen.

One afternoon as I was alone in my hospital room looking out the window at a beautiful day I began to feel dizzy and had trouble breathing. In addition to all the discomfort in my body I suddenly felt exceptionally weak and faint. My attempt to reach for the nurse's call button was in vain. I could barely move and genuinely felt like I was dying right then and there. I don't remember feeling fearful, only wondering whether to resist or just surrender. Then suddenly I was aware of movement. It was me in my body, lifting up from the bed toward the ceiling! How could this be when, at the same time, I also clearly saw my body lying on the bed? In an instant I saw and felt myself standing upright and yet not really touching on what looked like a floor of light. I was moving quickly yet at the same as if in slow motion, floating effortlessly along a wide corridor filled with soft, radiating white light and being aware of having no pain, no anxiety, no struggle.

Feelings of absolute peacefulness entered and enveloped me. On either side of me were crowded rows and rows of very many people in an endless space of brilliant white light surrounded by exceptionally beautiful colors I had never before seen! I was amazed by everything I was experiencing and startled at how this space could be so crowded and yet I had the ability to see everyone. They were luminous with loving faces and bodies that were beautifully peaceful and translucent. They were all opening their arms to me, waving and smiling. I was being warmly welcomed and enfolded in tender love and acceptance. The wonderful feeling of this flowing through me was profoundly real. This was no dream.

Some of the light forms I saw were tall angelic beings. Some faces were vaguely familiar though I couldn't immediately place them. Then there were many others whom I instantly recognized. Young Diane, the very special girl about whom I wrote a story in this book, was in the front row beaming her lovely countenance to me. The beautiful 12 year old girl who had died in my arms, now smiling and holding her hands over her heart as I passed by. There to my amazement and delight was my very dear grandmother holding my sweet baby nephew in her light-filled arms. They were both smiling and even though I was still grieving their loss, I knew now beyond any doubt they were just fine. I saw my other wonderful grandparents and relatives, and a young cousin who had died when she was only 8 years of age. There were friends of my parents, former classmates, my former hospice patients, and patients I had cared for as a student nurse so many years earlier. I recognized them all.

One person was especially trying to get my attention by holding up and waving a white handkerchief with lace borders. I instantly remembered her. She was an elderly woman whom I had cared for in the hospital when I was a student. I had been assigned as her nurse every day for about two weeks. She was very ill and fragile and we both knew she was dying. I tried to keep her very comfortable. One day as I was about to go off duty she surprised me with a lovely gift she said she had made especially for me. It was a white hanky with lace edges that she had embroidered. I was very touched and wanted to accept her kind expression. However, there was a strict policy within hospital regulations. Nurses, especially students, were forbidden to accept money or gifts of any kind from any patient. Although I did my best to gently explain this to my sweet patient, she reacted with confusion and sadness at my rejection. Seeing this made me feel awful so I struggled to justify going against the rules and accept it anyway. Just at that moment my nursing instructor came into the room and, seeing the gift in my hands, re-stated the rule to both my patient and myself. With a heavy heart I was required to return it. Before leaving the room with my instructor I made a heartfelt apology and whispered a thank you to my patient. I told this sweet woman I would see her the next day and she said, "Oh yes dear, we'll see each other again." She died that night. In my youth and inexperience I had missed the meaning and prophecy of her last statement.

In the 50+ years since then, that special memory had faded from my conscious mind. Now, as I was floating effortlessly along this glowing white light corridor here was my gracious patient reminding me of her promise that we would meet again. Yes indeed, I remembered her and gestured my delight at seeing her as she waved her gift to me - a lovely white handkerchief with hand-embroidered lace edges. I tried reaching for her outstretched hand yet my body just kept gliding along. I realized that my body was not solid like it had been in the hospital bed. It was translucent like everyone else's in this magnificent place. What an amazing experience of knowing I was floating on an ethereal plane of existence surrounded by so many familiar beings warmly welcoming me with grace and love.

I was in awe of the beauty, the peace and love in this place. At the far end of this corridor was an immense brilliant outpouring, an intense apex of pure White Light inviting me into Itself. I absolutely knew without any shred of doubt It was the Christ Light, the Divine Source, God. As I traveled nearer to the stunningly radiant, pure and shimmering glow of Light I wanted nothing more than to become totally enveloped in that exquisite Light of Supreme Unconditional Love. This was what it was to die and be almost Home. It was such an incredibly beautiful and easy transition! I kept gliding eagerly and effortlessly to the brilliant Light at the end of the hallway. Yes, I thought, I am ready to go and these people whom I had known, now in their own spirit form, were here to guide me. It felt so perfect in every way. I was almost there!

Then quite abruptly there was a dramatic shift! I was shocked to feel a sensation of moving backward, away from that brilliant Love Light which was quickly becoming more distant. Also, the many beautiful, smiling, and loving souls on either side of me began to fade from my vision. I could not reverse the motion. What was happening? "No! " I cried out, "don't let this end! I want to go to the Light!" Just then I very distinctly heard a powerful, commanding yet gentle Voice give me a strong directive. I clearly heard the words, "Not now, Jean. Go back. Shaun needs you." If I ever doubted the voice of God being truly heard out loud, those doubts immediately were erased. The power and love in this Voice could be no other.

As I began traveling backward at what felt like warp speed, I had a flood of emotion....confusion, fear, deep disappointment and loss, and then rapidly floating downward to the hospital bed where I saw my body lying. I felt myself move back into my body without my intention or permission, returning to the pain and weakness and sadness I had known before this ethereal experience. I was confused, frustrated, upset, and felt a great sense of loss. My body was trembling. What had just happened to me and why did I have to return to this suffering? Was it as real as it felt and as I believed it to be? What did the strange message mean? My son Shaun was 19 years old, in college, and he was fine! I was desperately trying to process all this and must have been crying because a nurse was standing beside me asking if I needed pain medication. I just stared at her and despite her caring presence I suddenly felt all alone and very lonely. I had just had a most profound spiritual experience that astounded me. Now I was back from it. What should I do now? Why did this happen? How could I speak of this to anyone? Who would understand? Who would even believe me? How and why would Shaun need me? It would be a few years before some of the answers became apparent. My disappointment and confusion about having to come back were challenging to overcome. At least I had assurance of my recovery which would enable me at some future time to fulfill the mysterious message about my son. Also, I had the vivid memory of my extraordinary out of body experience of floating in the spirit filled corridor toward that awesome heavenly Light of God.

On the practical side the process of getting fully well and understanding the metaphysical meaning for my illness was difficult, long and slow. Why had I allowed myself to become so depleted and vulnerable? Was this a type of self sabotage for decisions I had made or for the success of my career? Did I subconsciously feel I didn't deserve it? It was necessary to explore hidden recesses of my mind and heart that covertly held unresolved issues and unexpressed emotions. Journaling became an invaluable recourse for more honest expression and release of feelings that were still repressed due to fear, guilt, and shame. These went all the way back to the patriarchal rules of childhood. Learning to view myself as worthy and loveable during this time of deep personal soul searching was hard. I thought I had already mastered that. Oh, but the layers of a complicated life are deep and many.

Before all this happened I had immersed myself in therapy with efforts to become the best mother I could possibly be within a dissolving marriage and changing family dynamic. I had learned much about myself then. However, after my NDE I knew that self exploration at a deeper level was needed in becoming more fully well. I felt a spiritual responsibility to heal my whole self, not just to recover from the physical illness. I needed to manage myself and my life in gentler, more constructive ways. With time, dedication, patience and counseling, the struggle to understand became easier. I wanted to be the most clear and authentic holistic therapist and counselor for my clients that I could be. Also, I knew this was a necessary prelude to helping my son in whatever future ways I was meant to help.

It was 9 months before I was well enough to return to my private practice and feel confident and strong in my own authentic power. Of course I knew then, as now, that as long as we live in the physical dimension there will always be the need and opportunity for more growth, understanding, clarity, and truth in living from the depth of one's authentic being. Those who accept this deep soul responsibility are often held to a higher standard because of their awareness of it. That may mean having to deal with and transcend more difficult challenges within the physical complexity of this world. Many times others do not understand this. They often question why those on a spiritual path would have challenges at all. Just because one is on their spiritual path does not exempt that person from typical human reactions and susceptibility to illness. As long as we are on this earth plane we are subject to its human conditions of contrast and duality. Our journey through life is toward learning how to utilize those conditions in ways to attain spiritual enlightenment and wholeness. When we have accomplished completion of that goal we no longer need to return to this dimension of reality. During my recovery I was confronted by someone who was critical and belittling of my beliefs. That person asked in a mocking tone, "How did you allow yourself to become so sick? You should have known better or at least how to heal yourself." I answered, "My name is Jean, not Jesus. Jesus fulfilled His goal. I have not yet fulfilled mine so I'm still on the path, and He is right here with me, as the Christ Light." Affirming that truth out loud strengthened me.

My eventual return to work was exciting. I enjoyed working again in deeper ways with my former clients and in welcoming new ones. My professional fields and contacts expanded with fresh opportunities. These presented themselves in various areas including new trainings and certifications, cross country travel, and my creation and public presentations of new classes and workshops, totaling 22 in all. My ability to see and feel auras and energy fields increased. Sensing the presence of my spirit guides and angels all around me was even more prominent.

As for my son Shaun, he graduated from college with a degree in engineering. I was happy he was open to learning from me the techniques of positive affirmations and visualizations to help him find just the right job position. I wasn't sure if this was the fulfillment of my strange near death message that "Shaun needs you" but it didn't matter. I was in a good place to readily help Shaun and his older brother Dennis in any way I possibly could. In time Shaun was settled in a very good job and was married to his high school sweetheart with a baby on the way. Dennis was doing very well, was married to a lovely young woman, and truly enjoying his job as a skilled airline pilot. Life was flowing well for my sons. My heart is forever full of love and pride for them.

In 1999 I eagerly awaited the birth of my son Shaun's baby, my first grandchild. The baby was due in August but he surprised and concerned us all by arriving in May, 11 weeks prematurely. Due to the immediacy of his birth he was named Shaun. I remembered the Voice message 11 years earlier, "Not now, Jean. Go back. Shaun needs you." I could not have known then that there would be a second Shaun for me to help.

As soon as I saw my first grandchild as this very tiny and very fragile new life, I spontaneously began singing a song to him right then and there. The words and melody were literally forming in my mind faster than I could think and they just automatically flowed into my voice as I stood there in awe of him. I sang these words.....

"Welcome to the world my little one

Welcome to the world, my new grandson

You are so precious to me, my heart sings out joyfully

Grandma is so happy you chose to be

A very special gift to our family

Angels watching over you, keeping you safe and strong

Whispering how we love you so, waiting to take you home

Welcome to the world my little one

Welcome to the world my new grandson

You are so precious to me, my heart songs out joyfully

I love you, Shaun Stuart Daly."

I sang this song repeatedly to him and added many prayers along with the channeling of healing energy to him. I did this continuously whenever I was with him and also when I was away from him. Prayer and healing energy sent with loving intention flow out to wherever the receiver is at any moment. Baby Shaun had so many prayers and love going out to him from his parents, grandparents, all his family and many other people. He was in the neonatal intensive care unit for 2 months and carefully monitored at home for another year. When he arrived home I changed the one lyric from "waiting to take you home" to "happy to have you home" and continued the healing energies.

Today Shaun is nearly 18 years old, fully healthy, handsome, tall, kind, caring, respectful, an honor student, and a 2nd degree Black Belt in Karate. Grandson Shaun also remembers this song. At age 3 he actually asked me to sing to him the song about the angels. I thought he meant a Christmas song so I began to sing one. He shook his head so I sang another. He said "No, Grandma, not those, I'll show you." He started to sing. I was shocked at how he was able to repeat word for word with the exact melody, the song that I sang to him during his first hours and first year of life. What is even more amazing is that we recently sang this song together and he sang it perfectly, at age 17. I'm proud to have his full permission to say this and to tell his story.

Both my son Shaun and my grandson Shaun have triumphed over various life challenges for which I feel grateful and privileged to have been here to assist them whenever they needed me.

My incredible out of body journey is as vivid to me now as it was 28 years ago. I certainly had no fear of death then and I have no fear of death now, nor will I ever have. The entire NDE experience with its many aftermaths of enriching blessings in my life has been very profound and I am deeply grateful. I've had many opportunities to assist others in knowing that life after death continues in a spiritually glorious way, that the transition is gentle and loving, that we are welcomed with an immensely embracing Love and there is no need at all to be afraid. Whenever it is truly my time to be totally enfolded in that splendid radiant Light, I know my work here will be finished and I shall happily embrace the welcoming transport to life in that exquisite spirit/soul dimension. Of course I know from my experience in 1988 that there will be wonderful new adventures for me to explore......helping others from what some refer to as "the other side." I prefer to call it my true, original Divine Home Base. Thank you God, for such an affirming and wondrous glimpse and for the richness of blessings from it.

THE MONROE INSTITUTE

With permission from the Monroe Institute, I share the words below that attracted me to attend their Gateway Voyage Program in May, 2013. The stories that follow are three of my true and most incredible experiences during the Monroe Institute's Gateway Voyage Program.

The Monroe Institute, an organization originated in 1974 by Robert A. Monroe and his research team, provides experiential education programs facilitating the personal exploration of human consciousness. Over the last 40 + years, tens of thousands of people have attended the Institute's residential and outreach programs, and millions have benefited from its educational materials. The Institute admits students of any race, color, creed, and national or ethnic origin.

The Monroe Institute also serves as the core of a research affiliation investigating the evolution of human consciousness and making related information available to the public. The Institute is devoted to the premise that focused consciousness contains solutions to the major issues of human experience.

A greater understanding of such consciousness can be achieved through coordinated research efforts using an interdisciplinary approach. For this reason the Institute is working in collaboration with researchers and clinicians in many areas, especially through university and clinical collaborations and its Professional membership and Board of Advisors.

There is a wealth of information on Robert Monroe and the Monroe Institute online and in bookstores.

A description of the program I attended at Monroe is as follows.

GATEWAY VOYAGE PROGRAM - 2013

You Are More Than Your Physical Body... Explore Who You Are and What is Possible!

THE GATEWAY VOYAGE

Experience a 5-day/6-night voyage of self-discovery using Hemi-Sync® audio-guidance technology. Experience Robert Monroe's original, ground-breaking program on the Exploration of Human Consciousness.

Gain a Deeper Understanding of Yourself.
Make Better Decisions and Create New Possibilities.

For over 40 years, thousands of people have participated in the Gateway Voyage program and experienced

exceptional states of consciousness and life-changing benefits.

During this program I had no preconceived idea, no expectation of what would or could happen during the deep meditations that expanded my consciousness to higher realms of awareness and abilities. I felt completely safe at all times and am profoundly grateful for the exploration of dimensions beyond the physical.

I share three of my most profound experiences which I have collectively entitled "Soul Rescues."

Trilogy of Soul Rescues

#1 *Together Again*

I was following the directives of the Gateway Program at the Monroe Institute in Faber, VA in May of 2013. As students in the weeklong intensive training, we had just been instructed in the method of entering the expanded consciousness state called Focus 21 through the use of Dr. Monroe's Hemi-Sync method. The explanation of this can be found at the Monroe Institute's website. It was a deep meditative experience toward which we had been advancing in our daily progressive sessions. We were guided to allow ourselves to be open to the natural flow of higher vibrational energy that was safe with positive spiritual intent and preparation. We were told there may be an experience of out of body travel yet to not attach to any specific expectation of one. I was skeptical that I could achieve that level yet hopeful that I at least would go into a deep state of meditation.

I set my intention to be open, went to the Focus 21 state of consciousness and found myself immersed in the lovely sensation of flying. Soon I was aware of hovering over a very large straw hat which I realized was on the head of a young woman who appeared to be Vietnamese or Chinese. She was distraught and crying, darting her eyes left and right as she hurried down a street of chaotic activity and gunfire with people running and yelling in their native dialect. Although I did not understand the language I soon knew from the scene that this was a war zone, the Vietnam War. This upset young woman seemed lost and bewildered and was weakly calling out a name. I presented myself as gently as I could to say that I was there to help her. Before she even showed me her abdominal gunshot wound I felt a deep physical pain in my own right side and gasped with the acuteness of it. I felt my physical hand fly to my right side trying to ease the searing discomfort but then I realized it was not mine and it suddenly released from me. Everything was so very clear and real yet I knew this was way beyond my usual three dimensional consciousness. I looked again at the young woman aside me who was grimacing in pain and holding her right side. She told me her name was Soo Ling, age 27 and she was looking for her husband Hoon, age 29. They had been married only 1 and 1/2 years and she was desperate to find him. That was when I knew instinctively that both of them were really dead yet they did not know it. They were still earth bound and had not yet crossed over into Spirit.

I told Soo Ling that I would take her to where she needed to go. I wasn't sure how I actually knew that. It just was so natural that I did. Suddenly we were on an old wooden bridge that stretched over murky water and was surrounded by abandoned, burnt out buildings. Across the bridge we saw a man in soldier's clothing limping along alone, obviously injured and weak. Soo Ling cried out that the man was her husband, Hoon.

She called out his name repeatedly until he looked up and recognized her with a stunned look on his face. The injured couple staggered toward each other and embraced, crying and trying to soothe one another. As they looked at me and looked around at the deserted scene, they slowly realized they had both been fatally injured and were in a time warp of expanded consciousness in between dimensions. They were shocked and bewildered as to what to do next. I said I'd take them to where they now belonged. They nodded in agreement and at that moment a beautifully brilliant beam of white light radiated down in a welcoming invitation to them. Happy to be together again, they joined hands in a loving clasp. They bowed to me in respectful acknowledgement as they were escorted by angelic beings and lifted fully into the Light of God. It was an astonishing sight to behold.

I came out of that deep meditative state and immediately wrote down every detail. I was relaxed and comfortable yet excited, truly amazed, and very thankful for having such an incredible experience. The powerful meaning of what had just occurred deepened in my awake consciousness throughout the rest of the day. I later learned that this is known as soul rescue, a powerful yet gentle and loving assistance to those who need help crossing over. What a gift to know, through this incredibly real experience, that there is yet another way to help others, through a dimension beyond our earthly third one, a way that assists them in returning in Love and Light to their original spiritual Home.

#2 *The Story of Christopher Mellon*

I was once again following the directives of the Gateway Program at the Monroe Institute in Faber, VA in May of 2013 and was able to enter into the expanded consciousness state of Focus 21. When I arrived there I once again found myself experiencing out of body travel and the lovely sensation of flying. As I scanned the landscape below me I clearly saw a young boy standing on the bank of a river against a large old tree. The tree's trunk was gaping open with a deep wound as if it had been hit by lightning long ago. I saw that the young boy was alone and seemed quite forlorn as he played with a stick, drawing circles in the thick mud of the river bank. At times he would nestle into the comforting shelter of the aged tree perhaps seeking to ease his bewilderment and deep loneliness. His clothes were old and worn and appeared to be from an earlier time period, which I somehow knew was 1841. His hair was thick and brown, resembling a mop top style. His large brown eyes held a haunting lonely sadness. I gently approached him so as not to frighten him and said hello. He looked at me and said in a melancholy and faltering voice that he didn't know where he was, or why he was alone or where he should go. After introducing myself I assured him that I was there to help him, that he would be safe and that he could trust me. He said he was Christopher Mellon, was 6 years old, lived in Little Falls, Wisconsin, and repeated that he was lost, didn't know where he was, how he had gotten there, or what to do. He didn't know how long he had felt bewildered, desolate and confused.

Suddenly in my peripheral vision I saw what looked like a huge vat of cornmeal or grain. I began physically choking and coughing and was unable to breathe. I felt very scared. Then as suddenly as this feeling began it stopped. My over-whelming realization was that Christopher Mellon had died by choking and suffocation when he fell into a silo or a vat on a farm, probably at or near where he had lived. I was stunned to realize that just as with the couple in my first Focus 21 state, this boy was dead. He was in between worlds and I was here to help him cross over.

As I comforted him I told him that I would take him to where he now belonged and people who love him would be waiting for him. He smiled and appeared very relieved. At that moment a soft yet brilliant beam of white light shimmered and shone in the near distance with a gently welcoming energy. I took Christopher's hand and led him toward the Light. His face was aglow with surprise and delight. I could feel the relaxation and comfort expand within him. He knew he was safe and I knew he was ready to go. As we walked toward the radiant Light I saw several pure shining images....translucent, angelic-like beings.... who were waiting to welcome and receive him. Before he disappeared into the Light this beautiful child smiled, waved and said goodbye to me. I was filled with a tremendous vibration of deep love and trust, the Presence of God.

As I verbalized this second amazing story of rescue to the others in my Gateway group, my eyes filled with tears and my heart was full of gratitude. They too shared my emotions. I've always had a special affinity for children so to be able to help this young boy was particularly meaningful to me. Christopher Melon was finally and truly at peace to enjoy happiness and new life in his Spiritual Home.

#3 *Finding Becky Brown*

By now, in my third travel, it was becoming easier to enter the Hemi Sync expanded consciousness state of Focus 21. I went immediately into that state, out of my body, and was again experiencing the lovely sensation of flying. This time I saw a sparsely populated wooded area which opened up to the scene of a white clapboard house somewhere in Tennessee or perhaps Alabama. There in the front yard was a baby girl standing alone in a make shift playpen. I was fascinated by the structure of it. This enclosure was suspended with ropes between 2 sturdy trees. It had a wooden floor with a 3 feet tall creation of braided rope to make the 4 sides which were stretched between wooden poles in each corner. The baby girl looked to be about 2 years of age. She was wearing a red and white checkered sunsuit with white cotton lace embroidered around the bib of the outfit, just like the ones worn by children in the 1950's. This sweet child appeared to be confused and scared, sucking her thumb and looking nervously around her. Her skin was very pale and her eyes appeared hollow. As I moved closer to this little girl I instinctively knew her name was Becky Brown. She responded immediately yet wordlessly to this name when I called to her. The look on her little face was a mixture of relief and hope. I felt sad for her. She was alone. In trying to reassure and calm her I told her I would take care of her and asked her where Mommy and Daddy were. She began to whimper and point. I followed her finger direction and was startled to see a burned out automobile with 2 people lying dead on the ground next to the car. Without a doubt I clearly knew that the man and woman were Jack and Rita Brown, Becky's parents. I called to them and they responded with a dazed and questioning look. After introducing myself and telling them I was there to help them, they asked me if they were still alive. I gently told them no, that their bodies, along with their baby girl's, had died in the explosion yet their spirits were alive and waiting to transcend this world into their spiritual home. I would take them, together with their daughter, to that most special place where they all now belonged.

At that moment a beautiful and now familiar shaft of brilliant white Light opened to receive them into Its welcoming love and peace. As Becky's parents picked up and embraced their precious baby girl I escorted them all to the Light, adorned with shimmering angelic beings to guide them. I witnessed the Brown family glide effortlessly together into their new spiritual life. How humbly honored and thankful I felt to be able to once again assist in the journey of earthly beings to their souls' heavenly home.

Later, I wondered how Becky had died. Was she in the car and thrown from an explosion that landed her in the playpen? Was she hurriedly put in there by her parents as they sensed a sudden serious problem with the car? I felt that she had to be killed along with them even though her body was in a different location.

As I tried to figure it out I was reminded by my own spiritual guidance that it didn't really matter. The real importance of my out of body experience was that I had fulfilled the purpose of it.......rescuing the three souls of a family from the confusion of being in-between worlds to the clarity, safety, beauty, love, peace, purity and Light of their Spiritual Home.

These amazing 'soul rescue' experiences have profoundly impacted my own soul and heart in a deeper and richer understanding of life's continuing existence of our Living Spirit and the unwavering eternal connection with our Creator.

It makes me smile to know that my lifetime mission of helping others, especially in my 50+ years of nursing, has expanded and evolved into another dimension of continued life. Thank you, God for this extraordinary privilege.

The Robins' Gift

I was living and working alone, engaged in private practice as a holistic nurse therapist, counselor, and educator. One of the many modalities I used to help people was the channeling of healing energy through the method known as Reiki, which has been described in other parts of this book. Although I was quite busy with a continual flow of clients, I began feeling unsure about the true effectiveness of my energy work on some of my patients who were suffering from very serious and debilitating illnesses. A few of them did not seem to respond the way I had hoped. It surprised me that I was feeling such insecurity and doubt. After all, I believed that I was simply the open channel for this God Source Universal Energy. I was well trained in how to channel it with sincere intent and trust that it would go to where and how it was needed and accepted by each individual. Although I truly desired to see all my clients respond each time with major relief of pain and distress, it was not up to me as the channel to decide how and when that should be. My work was that of a facilitator to reconnect my clients to their own innate abilities for healing and wholeness. My mind and spirit knew that, yet my heart and human ego longed to see them more comfortable after I had ministered to them. I knew it was necessary for me to let go of my own expectations of certain healing outcomes but doing that was not always easy. I was struggling to totally release my old subconscious fear of not being good enough. I began to question the possibility of needing more training even though I had been doing energy work since 1972 with much success in helping people achieve their goals of healing in the many holistic ways it can unfold.

My desire was for an obvious sign that I was still making a truly meaningful and positive difference in those people whose suffering seemed so severe. I also wanted to be certain that I was meant to continue doing what I had believed was my soul mission. I found myself longing for an actual demonstration and validation from God.

My daily work with clients continued as I repeatedly reminded myself to trust in the Universal Order of things without interjecting my ego into how things "should" be, yet I was still hopeful that in some way at some time my prayers for reassurance would be heard. I could not have imagined then, the astonishing way in which the answer would be revealed.

During this time there was one entire week that passed with a steady, chilly spring rain. It saturated everything and cast a penetrating gloom over the entire neighborhood. At times the outer gloom renewed my inner self-doubts and I'd pray again to stop the ego intrusions into my work.

Finally the rain ended and the sun began to shine once again. I was glad to resume my daily routine of an early morning walk, thankful for the warmer air and brighter sky. It was on that first walk when I noticed a beautiful robin lying very still on the side of the road near my home. Was she dead? I peered more closely and saw that she was just barely alive. Her breaths were nearly imperceptible. I felt I could not leave her to suffer so I ran home to find a box and some towels for cushioning and returned to gently lift her into the box. I could not see any distinctly broken parts of her body, although one wing appeared torn and her neck and one leg both looked contorted. This poor creature had to be in pain and needed help.

I carried the desperately weak bird home, placed the box on my porch and sat with the her as I automatically opened myself to be a channel of healing. I wasn't sure what else I could do so I called an emergency veterinarian's office. My car was in the repair shop so taking her there was not an option. The doctor told me that she would most likely die very soon but I could try to offer water. I began intervals of channeling Reiki to this delicate robin every 15 minutes, talking to her, and offering water which she was unable to receive. I called on every heavenly being for assistance. The least I could do was to comfort and ease her during her dying process. For the first hour I saw no change but was encouraged that at least she was still alive. In the second hour I began to see more regular breathing and some minor movements in her with a slight shifting of her head and an ability to take some water from my finger. I prayed and continued the Reiki energy while encouraging this sweet bird with my words. Perhaps it was not her time to die just then. That was not up to me. I needed to be focused on channeling healing for her comfort and ease, and give her reassurance of being loved and cared for no matter the outcome, whether she lived longer or died soon. I reminded myself that this was how I had ministered to my hospice patients some years earlier. It was really the best attitude for every person and being to whom I offered help.

Into the third hour the small struggling robin was trying to flutter her wings and attempting to move about. To my total surprise both her neck and leg began to assume more normal positions. I called back the veterinarian's office with this exciting news and asked what food bit I could offer if it was at all possible for her to eat it. He said a worm or insect or even a tiny nip of ground meat would be best, although he was definitely not optimistic that she could manage to take in any food. He was very surprised that she was still alive. Fortunately, I had some cooked ground turkey that was left over from the prior night's dinner so that was my first choice for this robin's food.

After 3 hours of ministering healing and nursing care I was delighted that my fragile patient began taking more water and was able to gradually eat a few morsels of the turkey meat. Little by little she was gaining strength. I didn't know exactly what this meant. I had often seen hospice patients gain abilities and strength right before they died as a final salute to their life and then die with ease and peace. Maybe that was what I was witnessing in this injured bird.

After another half hour I was amazed to witness this beautiful robin beginning to stand up, though a bit wobbly at first. Slowly she began to chirp and flutter. Within twenty minutes of standing up she was gingerly hopping around in the box. She would rest then begin again. Ten minutes after she began hopping she flapped her wings a few times. Even the torn wing showed a new strength. My excitement and confidence grew yet I was not at all prepared for her next action. To my complete amazement she suddenly stood tall and erect and right before my eyes, she flew up into the sky. I was astounded at her apparent complete recovery as I watched her gliding through the blue sky circling high above my home with clearly outstretched strong wings! My heart was filled with gratitude for this bird's healing.

I realized that this was a demonstration of the reassurance I had sought yet I had never expected it to look like this! It was a validation that had restored full belief in my ability to lovingly do all I can to help, while letting go of specific expectations for the outcome and an assurance that my work in helping others was to be continued. I felt very appreciative.

I thought this robin's amazing flight was the end of my story....... until the next morning. While preparing breakfast I became aware of an unusually loud chirping melody that definitely sounded like a multitudinous bird song. It was strange that the sound persisted at a very high decibel level so I followed it to the front of my house and opened the door. There to my utter astonishment were what appeared to be at least 100 robins standing in a group on my front porch, filling the entire space. They were all chirping at the same time in a harmonious chorus, looking right at me and bobbing their heads! Although I was dumfounded at this sight, the thought immediately came to me that they were there in a display of gratitude for the healing and return of their friend. Just as that knowing resonated in my mind the robins suddenly became silent all at once. They stood there in silence for a very long incredible moment looking at me in what felt like a respectful acknowledgement. Then to my amazement they all nodded to me in unison and together in one beautiful sweep, flew up and away into the sky, creating a perfect circular pattern over my house. For several moments I couldn't move, not able to believe what I had just heard and seen. I had never known of or even imagined anything like this before, much less experienced it myself!

It was a truly magnificent gift from the robins to me that still to this day 22 years later fills my soul and heart with gratitude and joy. In a most unexpected and profound way I had received confirmation in my abilities to help others through my intentional partnership with Spirit and by trusting that each soul knows the perfect outcome for itself according to its purpose here. The birds' exemplary gift to me represented the truth that even as individual creations, we are ALL truly united in Spirit. Sharing love, compassion, respect, and healing with each other and with nature are essential threads in weaving a beautiful tapestry of living life together, shared by all in peace and harmony, a life that is our Divine heritage.

Angels Answering the Call

I was alone while driving on a 3 lane state highway about 5 p.m. It was dark and foggy with a cold misty rain, often changing into sleet. I was traveling below the speed limit of 65 MPH due to the weather and heavy traffic, which was an oddity at that time since it was a Sunday. While driving in the middle lane I noticed a car to my left drifting over the line into my lane. The young driver was on a cell phone. I slowed up, gave a light beep to him as an alert to pay attention and move over. He remained where he was. Due to traffic I was not able to move into the right lane. The young man was still drifting over, barely ahead of me. Suddenly, I felt a chill go up my spine as I heard some loud sounds in the distance. Although I have a habit of thanking my guardian angels everyday for always being with me, I now felt a strong urgency to ask them for extra safely and protection on the road. A few seconds later the road inclined and became more slick. The same car that had been drifting over into my lane was now in front of me. In an instant I saw and heard it swerve and slam into another car ahead of us. That car had already crashed into the concrete barrier and was sitting sideways in the middle of the highway. There were other vehicles also which had apparently approached the incline too fast, were too close to each other, and slid out of control on the slick road.

The darkness, icy rain, fog, slick road incline, and unprepared drivers all contributed to creating conditions for a spontaneous multi-car involvement. It was a horrific accident scene that kept replaying with cars in front of me, behind me, and aside me crashing into each other all around me. What a shocking sight to suddenly come upon and then instantly be part of! My immediate challenge was to somehow stay in control of my car while trying to avoid the other ones. It was to no avail. I jolted to a stop, ending up sideways in the passing lane. There was literally nowhere to go. I was trapped and afraid of being killed or severely injured. My body was trembling and my prayers for help became more urgent. I squeezed my eyes shut and braced myself for impact by another oncoming car screeching in its attempts to stop. Amazingly, it did not strike me.

All of a sudden I became aware of my car blindly moving forward while still turned sideways in the chaotically cluttered road. My hands were locked on the steering wheel but they were not moving it. My eyes flew open. What was happening? It actually looked and felt like my car was being automatically driven or led by some invisible force across 2 lanes, somehow as if by magic, avoiding the mangled mess that littered the road. It was certainly not me driving the car. Glass and metal had been flying everywhere and yet, to my utter amazement, I was not touched and was actually feeling a strange sense of calm. It felt dream-like as I then found myself stopped with my car against and evenly parallel to the guardrail on the opposite side of the highway. I had no idea how I ended up there. It was a miracle that I was not hit by a car nor had I hit anyone else nor had I hit the guardrail, even though my car was less than a half inch from it. I was stunned.

As I once again realized the accident scene all around me and heard people screaming, I shook myself out of the trance-like stupor, found my cell phone and started to call 911. Being a nurse I wanted to help anyone that was hurt but I couldn't open my door or get out of the car. I implored angels to help everyone there. Suddenly, and again as if by magic, there appeared in the middle of this dire situation a very large, tall black man in a bright white coat and pants. I remember thinking how odd he looked there and how strange that he just appeared out of nowhere in the center of it all. Where did he come from? Despite the rain, fog, and darkness of the night this man was standing in a pure white spotlight that emanated from above him and radiated out from him in all directions, casting a bright white light on the entire scene. He stood with his arms outstretched and his large hands held high. In a loud commanding voice he was ordering cars to stop as they started to come over the incline. They all came to an immediate and dramatic halt. The man stood in place, not moving, and seemed to be impenetrable. Nothing and no one touched him. Although people were still screeching to a stop there were no more crashes. I remember being amazed and also confused, wondering who he was and where he came from. All of this must have taken only a minute or two even though it seemed that everything was in slow motion. Then there was a momentary eerie quiet and absolute stillness all around.

It was then that this large black man in bright white clothing came over to me and kindly told me to stay in the car and that he'd get me out of there. He did not want me to wait for the police. With a wave of his large hands and never entering my car, he somehow miraculously got me out of the way by perfectly guiding me in-between the stopped cars and the mangled road mess. Had I been the one driving? When my car came to a stop I found myself sitting behind the steering wheel with hands in my lap, realizing I was on the highway's shoulder well beyond the center of the accident scene. I had no idea how that could have happened. I felt as though I had been in another dimension. Thankfully, the sirens were blaring so I knew others would be promptly taken care of. I looked back to find the large tall man in bright white clothing but I could not see him or the light surrounding him amid police cars and ambulances. It was all so surreal. He had simply disappeared. There was no explanation other than he must have been an angel sent to help. I had indeed called on the angels yet as far as I could tell I had not ever in this lifetime experienced such a powerful angelic being in real human form.

I sat in my car for a while processing this miraculous

event. As the memory replayed in my mind I felt shaken and needed to settle myself. I realized that my son Dennis' house was close by. When I had the courage to drive again I went there to recover from the ordeal and share my incredible story. What a comfort to be met at the door by my then 9 year old sweet granddaughter with her loving hug and offers of rest, aspirin, and hot tea, as she and her parents listened to my mystical experience.

I believe I was given a miracle. I was the only car <u>not</u> hit. There was not even a scratch on my car although I had been surrounded by many who couldn't stop in time. I learned that, despite the very forceful impacts in the multi-car accident, no one had died or was seriously injured. I believe that the angels I had called on for extra protection did protect and help not only me but everyone involved.

Throughout all time the message from angels has always been that they are always available to help us. They are God's special intermediaries and all we need to do is call upon them. This time they even sent a very special angel looking like a doctor dressed in a white coat and pants and wearing a "head light." Of course he must have had his wings hidden under the coat! Here was another amazing demonstration of Divine Power I shall remember forever. Once again I am deeply and forever grateful for God's angels answering my call.

EPILOGUE

During the writing of this book I wanted to interject many concepts I learned and came to believe as spiritual truths. Some are already included in certain contexts throughout each story. These felt important for me to share in more detail yet I realized that to do so during the writing would interrupt the flow of my personal stories. I present them here for better clarity and understanding of my experiences. Some may be unintentionally repetitive.

So, my dear reader, with respect for your own individual life path and choices, I hope these can somehow be helpful to you or at least interesting, whether or not you share a personal belief in these concepts.

My first major authentic truth is that we are spiritual beings having human experiences. I believe we were each created from pure Love as beings in the Image and Likeness of our Creator. We were given free will and choice to explore and experience life on Earth with its physical dimensions of time and space. The energy frequencies of our world are much lower in vibration and density than the highest absolute purity of God energy. When we chose to enter the physical dimension the plan was to explore, experience, learn and return. We carried within us the eternal imprint of our Divine spiritual origin and core truths with the promise to remember them and use them for guidance, inspiration and our eventual way Home.

So with our free will we consciously chose to enter this physical world of duality and contrast for the experience of it and all its emotions. It was to be a temporary, earthly dimension type of separation with the held-in-place memory of our Divine nature and perpetual connection with the Creator. Yet through the ages we, as a human species, allowed ourselves to become so deeply mired and fixated in this physical world that we began to believe that the physical was the true reality. We allowed our human ego to have undisciplined control. This resulted in forgetting, even denying, the real Truth that we are IN the world, NOT OF the world, that we are OF the Divine. Spiritually, we are all united as ONE, intricately connected by One Supreme Creator, no matter our various physical, mental, emotional, social, financial, environmental, cultural differences. However, over time and with increasing allegiance to human ego control rather than to spiritual truth, we became distant, alienated, even severed from the idea of oneness and unity.

I do know the idea of "oneness with all" seems to many people to be completely ridiculous, a totally unrealistic fantasy, or just plain crazy. I've been a first-hand receiver of this sarcasm and criticism and I understand why. We cannot even imagine being 'one' with people we consider being abhorrent to us. Also, the utter chaos and atrocities in our world can very strongly and justifiably defy and deny the goal of unity as having any possibility at all. Conflicts of power and control, rampant disrespect, greed, hatred, fear, violence, war and cruel inhumanity appear to reign supreme in many areas of the world and within the narrow, rigid minds and cold, vindictive hearts of many. It appears we are as far away from unity and peace as we can be. This is clearly seen in current political divisiveness and its effects in society. Even some organized religions espouse this competitive attitude.

Regardless of all this, every single thing in the entire universe is interconnected and made up of pure creative energy. This was one of my areas of study and is explained in depth by the science of quantum physics. Each creation, including each one of us, has its own electromagnetic energy field of certain vibratory frequencies. These are able to be influenced by vibrations of other frequencies that surround it, because of our connection. That means our thoughts, beliefs, words and emotions influence our own as well as others' vibrations to react and change to higher or lower frequencies. The lower the vibrations, the more dark, dense, fearful and heavy. The higher the vibrations, the more light, pure, loving and spiritual. Similar vibrations create mass consciousness. Mass consciousness is like a huge cloud that fills up with the vibrations of similar thoughts and expressions until it becomes so full that it must spill out into the physical world. The result and impact in one's life and on our planet is either negative or positive with the intensity being reflective of the type and density of vibrations. So paying close attention to the way we think, feel, behave and react empowers us to re-create our personal reality by choice, thus affecting a change in ourselves and in mass consciousness.

The old world paradigms of separation, egotistical power and control through fear and violence are of very low vibrations. The heavy density of these lowest vibrations has had a stronghold in our world for centuries and appears now to be reaching a planetary climax. We see it escalating in so many areas. This climax urgently summons the universal call for planetary and personal transformation from the release of fear and separation to alignment with love and unity. Thankfully, the call is being heard. It is a present fact that these very low vibrations, usually referred to as intense negativity, are now slowly being diluted, dissolved and transformed, bit by bit. This is being done by millions of people, often known as lightworkers, through their massive worldwide outpourings of loving intention, forgiveness, healing, kindness, prayer, meditation, visualization, affirmation, community support, etc. I believe we also have innumerable legions of God's angelic beings here to support and assist us in this effort, even as they must simultaneously respect our free will. Free will can be a tricky thing for us. Each choice we make exercises free will. We determine a choice based on either love or fear, both of which are humanity's main ruling emotions. Every other emotion is derived from those.

I've come to believe that peace can only come through living from our authentic and loving spiritual nature in the midst of experiencing human life with all its contrast and diversity. Those who resist this Divine Truth and live only from their egocentric mindsets continue to engage in the dark, low vibrations of distortion, fear, hatred, greed and war. Staying in those only breeds more of the same. These distortions are very dense and have a powerfully negative and infectious impact on society. Each person needs to take responsibility to avoid succumbing to this harmful and divisive negativity. We accomplish this by realizing that each one of us contributes in our own way, no matter how small, to these conflicts. Some examples may be sarcasm, bullying, revenge, rudeness, unkindness, mean-spiritedness or holding grudges. We can seek to deliberately recognize how we may be contributing in day to day life and relationships. This usually involves humbling oneself and owning up to that personal contribution. The next step is forgiveness of self and others followed by accepting individual responsibility for making changes that contribute to new ways of living in respect, love, peace and harmony. We can do this by intentionally raising our vibrations through thoughts, words, and actions to the more powerful energy forces of love. This is a disciplined choice. It is learning to live from the inside out..... from our spiritual soul to our physical expression....a lifelong process to follow.

Throughout history every great spiritual leader, especially the one known best to me as the Master Jesus Christ, taught us that love, kindness, compassion and forgiveness are the truest and most powerful qualities of healing and peace. They raise our vibrations to a more highly refined spiritual level above the fray. These qualities have a very powerful positive impact and offer the ability to see beyond the chaos to a path of reorganization. This creates a holistic perspective and a new blueprint for healing. Healing requires tolerance, acceptance, respect, patience, love and peace, in spite of the appearance of man-made chaos. This path leads to the remembrance of our unity and oneness with God and each other. We need to look toward, remained focused on, and believe in that outcome. It may not be easy yet we can make conscious choices every day to act out these spiritual qualities in ourselves and with each other. Everyone has at least some opportunity to regularly contribute, at the very least by sincere intention. Some examples are prayer and meditation, good deeds, tolerance, patience, understanding, acts of kindness and generosity, respectful, honest communications. Thankfully there are already millions of people on our planet now who make these daily positive choices individually and together. The positive intentions they set forth with these actions are immensely powerful. Look for them, expect them, and you'll find them. They are inspiring and uplifting.

To me it's so sad that worldwide media does not often portray these lightworkers as it desperately needs to do. Most of the focus in the news and in social media is rabid, detailed, damaging sensationalism of chaos, cruelty, rage and depraved violence. This repeated sensationalism represents the lowest of vibrations and promotes more of the same destructive action. What really needs to be shown repeatedly are examples of the millions of people worldwide who have been promoting peace and unity by being actively engaged in loving, sharing, caring actions of kind service every day. These need much more global representation on a continual, daily basis through all media channels. That would demonstrate how important it is that everyone contribute in their own good way. It would add positive energy to the mass consciousness. In this world we are either part of the problem or part of the solution. The best and most lasting solution always involves the spirit of love. Love is usually known as a positive, good feeling and it needs to be supported by action. The truest love is unconditional and is not always reciprocal, like that of a parent to their child. Also, love does not need to include condoning a person's actions or loving their human personality. It means recognizing and accepting their true spiritual nature and the same in ourselves. It means giving respect to that part of their being and to our own being. We can maintain a spirit of love even though we make a choice to detach from certain people and relationships. We can maintain a spirit of love and respect even though we disagree with others' belief systems, ideas, actions. Even when we feel hurt or angry or resentful because of someone's behavior we can utilize that to learn something valuable about ourselves which caused our own reaction. Often these instances can be our greatest teachers. In seeking a way to demonstrate love, we raise the vibrations of everyone and everything involved.

I once was shown these concepts in a vivid vision. I saw myself standing on a curb viewing with horror at a street brawl with many people involved. My focus was centered on the street mob, the garbage strewn around and people acting terribly violent to each other. By staring at the bedlam I could see nothing else and I felt very upset, angry, scared and helpless to do anything about it. The violent energy was intensifying and infecting the gathered crowd of spectators with many of them joining in the riot. Then in that vision I was suddenly lifted off the curb and up to the top of a building where I could still see the street brawl but I could also see other people on the periphery doing ordinary things like shopping, laughing, playing. With this expanded view I was able to include these other scenes in my experience, so my feeling of anger was somewhat lessened because of it. The street violence did not negate the happiness played out elsewhere. As I focused on those scenes I was able to feel calmer and then send out those calming energies to the people in the street. The final vision was of me high on a hilltop. Now I was able to see much more from that height and enjoy the beauty of the clear blue sky, the sunshine, the trees and flowers, the singing birds and expanses of beautiful landscape below. All of this loveliness surrounded both the people engaged in violence and the happy people in the distance.

It became clear that this visionary gift was a perfect example of perspective and my choice as to where I would focus my attention. By allowing my attention to be on all the positives I saw, I could raise my own energy vibration to feel calm, relaxed and centered. Then I was able to share all of those loving, compassionate, and healing energy vibrations with the people in that street. I saw myself directing a focused and very powerful beam of light and love into that scene. My intention to help in that way was the most powerful thing I could do. This is always helpful and effective in some way even if we cannot witness that effect at the time. Love is the most powerful vibratory energy force in the Universe. After all, the pure love of Divine Source is how we came into being.

Another thing I learned was that being in charge really meant becoming responsible for oneself, becoming more conscious of every thought, belief, feeling and action with the potential consequences of each. I realized that I had an inner power to change my thoughts in a way that would lead to honoring the God Source within me and within everyone and everything. Putting that power into actual daily life however, proved very challenging. Being the idealist I was, I thought that all I had to do was practice positive affirmations. I had yet to discover the unconscious self-defeating beliefs behind what I was trying to consciously create as positive outcomes. One of my mentors called this "the thought behind the thought." This means that individuals must discover the unconscious belief systems that contradict the conscious affirmations they are repeating. The conflict must be resolved before the positive affirmations can come into physical realization and manifestation.

Two simple examples would be:

1) Someone wanting to grow a garden. The person provides fertile soil, water, sunlight and weed control, yet at the same time thinks repeatedly that it won't be successful because they've not been

able to grow anything in the past. That belief can cancel out the result they want. Even if the garden does grow they may credit it to just being lucky and continue with the same negative belief system.

2) A person making daily affirmations of staying healthy and well. Someone in this person's family gets sick during the much advertised "cold and flu season." If the belief system has been that the illness will make the rounds to everyone else like it usually does, then the affirmer unconsciously waits for the illness to infect them saying they "knew it" and believes that affirmations just don't work. The strongly held unconscious belief system overrides the positive affirmation.

With every event, relationship, situation and condition in one's life there is a reason and a season, a beginning and an ending, a meaning and a purpose, whether or not we ever really know or understand. I have learned that a crisis in one's life can be the very thing that reveals a need for transformation or forgiveness within oneself that had been denied or ignored. It may be that the very person who causes you the most distress can be your best teacher for necessary self growth. To realize this takes some emotional maturity and lots of practice because our egos usually resist by telling us to judge and blame the other.

There are so many opportunities to stretch and reach for our highest potential. To give love to someone does not require friendship or approval of their actions. It requires recognition of their spiritual core connected with yours.

You can choose to move away from them. You can choose to not judge and instead send love energy to them and go on your way. It may be that later you will notice the blessing to yourself. We are all in this together, each one of us a work in progress.

Through connecting deeply with my spirituality, I am able to love, value and trust my core spiritual self to lead and guide me. Within my soul, the dwelling place of God, I strive to authentically live the purposes for which I was born, be they major or small, public, private or barely noticeable to others. I believe that God, the Eternal Creative Loving Energy Source, is within each soul and speaks to each of us all the time. We need to be very quiet and listen. As one of my favorite Bible quotes from Psalm 46:10 states, "Be Still and Know that I am God." Remembering this, I can simply BE in the moment and truly feel the beautiful and soothing shower of Divine grace and love, ever present to all. I believe we are meant to enjoy life in precious moments of time, to laugh and play amid the challenges, to recognize and delight in spontaneous serendipities and trust there are more along the way. I experience these very frequently now as I deliberately choose to be in the flow of Spirit. It is in this flow that miracles can and do happen. I am no more deserving than anyone else. We are all worthy. We just need to know that our worth and value originate from our Creator, and then choose to be in that flow, day after day.

Like the energy of the Universe our purpose here is multidimensional, multifaceted and continually unfolding and expanding. I believe that the soul lives forever. I also believe that we have free choice, after physical death, to re-enter the physical dimension in multiple lifetimes. The reasons for this choice can be many and varied. Choices can be made to further explore and experience this dimension for various reasons such as; correcting mistakes, balancing what is known as karma, completing unfinished purposes, re-living and better understanding human emotions and sensations, enjoying former relationships, helping and serving others who are struggling to know their spiritual core as their authentic self, or simply spreading unconditional love and joy.

In any lifetime our truest responsibilities are to get out of our own way, to be still and listen to the Voice of God within, to appreciate, be grateful and give thanks, to deeply love and easily forgive, and to take the next step, be it on the solid ground of knowing or in a flight of faith. As my very favorite inspirational song says, "Let There Be Peace on Earth and Let It Begin with Me."[1] And so the journey continues, on and on........

[1] Copyright 1955, 1983 by Jan-Lee Music (ASCAP.) Used by Permission; all rights reserved.